Contents

Licence

IMPORTANT – PERMITTED USE AND WARNINGS – READ CAREFULLY BEFORE USING

Text © Wendy Garner and Tony Pickford
© 2005 Scholastic Ltd

Published by Scholastic Ltd, Villiers House,
Clarendon Avenue, Leamington Spa,
Warwickshire CV32 5PR

Printed by Bell & Bain Ltd, Glasgow

3 4 5 6 7 8 9 0   8 9 0 1 2 3 4

British Library Cataloguing-in-Publication Data
A catalogue record for this book is available from
the British Library.

ISBN 0-439-97193-4

ISBN 978-0439-97193-5

**Visit our website at
www.scholastic.co.uk**

CD developed in association with
Footmark Media Ltd

Authors
Wendy Garner and Tony Pickford

Editor
Christine Harvey

Project Editor
Wendy Tse

Assistant Editors
Jane Gartside and Kim Vernon

Series Designer
Joy Monkhouse

Designer
Erik Ivens

Cover photographs
© DigitalVision/Getty Images

This book is dedicated to Ruth Ravenscroft.

Acknowledgements

Extracts from the National Curriculum for England © Crown copyright material is reproduced with the permission of the Controller of HMSO and the Queen's Printer for Scotland. Extracts from Programmes of Study from The National Curriculum reproduced under the terms of HMSO Guidance Note 8. © Qualifications and Curriculum Authority.

Thank you to Pete MacKay for assisting in the research and writing of 'An island home: Coll', and to Georgie Beasley for assisting in the writing of 'Travelling to the British Isles' capitals'.

Every effort has been made to trace copyright holders and the publishers apologise for any omissions.

Due to the nature of the web, the publisher cannot guarantee the content or links of any of the websites referred to. It is the responsibility of the reader to assess the suitability of websites.

The rights of Wendy Garner and Tony Pickford to be identified as the authors of this work have been asserted by them in accordance with the Copyright, Designs and Patents Act 1988.

Minimum Specifications:
PC: Windows 98 SE or higher
Processor: Pentium 2 (or equivalent) 400 MHz
RAM: 128 Mb
CD-ROM drive: 48x (52x preferred)

MAC: OS 9.2 (OSX preferred)
Processor: G3 400 MHz
RAM: 128 Mb
CD-ROM drive: 48x (52x preferred)

▶▶ List of resources on the CD-ROM

The page numbers refer to the teachers' notes provided in this book.

INTRODUCTION

This book and CD-ROM support the teaching and learning set out in the QCA Scheme of Work for geography in Years 1 and 2. The CD provides a large bank of visual and aural resources. The book provides teachers' notes, background information, ideas for discussion and activities to accompany the CD resources, along with photocopiable pages to support the teaching. All have been specifically chosen to meet the requirements for resources listed in the QCA units for Years 1 and 2. Some additional resources and ideas have also been included to enable teachers to develop and broaden these areas of study if they wish. These include activity sheets to help children clarify their thinking or record what they find out.

The resources and activities are not intended to provide a structure for teaching in themselves, but are designed to give a basis for discussion and activities which focus on the knowledge, skills and understanding required by the National Curriculum for geography. The children are encouraged to develop key skills such as observing, questioning, describing, sorting and sequencing.

Graphicacy is one of the key skills in geography and it covers all forms of pictorial communication of spatial information: ground-level photographs, oblique and vertical aerial photographs, diagrams, signs and symbols, and maps of all sorts – from pictorial to Ordnance Survey. Maps and their conventional use of plan view are important in geography, but children see their world from eye-level. There is a large conceptual leap between eye-level and plan (aerial) view so children can be helped to make sense of, and understand, the relationship between horizontal and vertical viewpoints by the use of intermediate perspectives, that is, views taken from a range of oblique angles.

Links with other subjects

Maths
Skills such as counting, measuring, matching, ordering and sequencing are essential to both geography and maths. Measuring skills are fostered when children calculate distances, and they learn to tell the time to work out how long journeys take.

Literacy
There are a number of close links between the units covered in this book and work on literacy. The discussion activities contribute directly to the requirements for speaking and listening. The information sheets could be used to provide a stimulus for shared, guided or independent reading. There is considerable opportunity for the children to develop their independent writing skills as they produce leaflets or write simple captions using the word cards. Pictures from the CD could be printed to stimulate independent writing, or to illustrate it.

History
Children learn about the history of a settlement in the study of a local area, in this case Chester, and the chapter on 'Going to the seaside' offers a look at what Tenby was like in the past. Learning about the history of buildings not only links with the way of life for people in the past, but also links with work on homes in the locality.

Science
The discussion of land use and geographical locations enable children to appreciate the variety of landscapes to be found in their own and contrasting areas.

HOW TO USE THE CD-ROM

Windows NT users
If you use Windows NT you may see the following error message: 'The procedure entry point Process32First could not be located in the dynamic link library KERNEL32.dll'. Click on **OK** and the CD will autorun with no further problems.

Setting up your computer for optimal use
On opening, the CD will alert you if changes are needed in order to operate the CD at its optimal use. There are three changes you may be advised to make:

Viewing resources at their maximum screen size
To see images at their maximum screen size, your screen display needs to be set to 800 x 600 pixels. In order to adjust your screen size you will need to **Quit** the program.

If using a PC, open the **Control Panel**. Select **Display** and then **Settings**. Adjust the **Desktop Area** to 800 x 600 pixels. Click on **OK** and then restart the program.

If using a Mac, from the **Apple** menu select **Control Panels** and then **Monitors** to adjust the screen size.

Adobe Acrobat Reader
To print high-quality versions of images and to view and print the photocopiable pages on the CD you need **Adobe Acrobat Reader** installed on your computer. If you do not have it installed already, a version is provided on the CD. To install this version **Quit** the 'Ready Resources' program.

If using a PC, right-click on the **Start** menu on your desktop and choose **Explore**. Click on the + sign to the left of the CD drive entitled 'Ready Resources' and open the folder called 'Acrobat Reader Installer'. Run the program contained in this folder to install **Adobe Acrobat Reader**.

If using a Mac, double-click on the 'Ready Resources' icon on the desktop and on the 'Acrobat Reader Installer' folder. Run the program contained in this folder to install **Adobe Acrobat Reader**.

PLEASE NOTE: If you do not have **Adobe Acrobat Reader** installed, you will not be able to print high-quality versions of images, or to view or print photocopiable pages (although these are provided in this book and can be photocopied).

It is recommended that certain images, such as maps and aerial views, are viewed and printed in **Adobe Acrobat Reader** as it will be easier to focus on specific areas.

QuickTime
In order to view the videos and listen to the audio on this CD you will need to have **QuickTime version 5 or later** installed on your computer. If you do not have it installed already or have an older version of QuickTime, the latest version can be downloaded at http://www.apple.com/quicktime/download/win.html. If you choose to install this version, **Quit** the 'Ready Resources' program.

PLEASE NOTE: If you do not have **QuickTime** installed you will be unable to view the films.

Menu screen
▶ Click on the **Resource Gallery** of your choice to view the resources available under that topic.
▶ Click on **Complete Resource Gallery** to view all the resources available on the CD.
▶ Click on **Photocopiable Resources (PDF format)** to view a list of the photocopiables provided in this book.
▶ **Back:** click to return to the **opening screen**. Click **Continue** to move to the **Menu screen**.
▶ **Quit:** click **Quit** to close the menu program and progress to the **Quit screen**. If you quit from the **Quit screen** you will exit the CD. If you do not quit you will return to the **Menu screen**.

Resource Galleries
▶ **Help:** click **Help** to find support on accessing and using images.
▶ **Back to menu:** click here to return to the **Menu screen**.
▶ **Quit:** click here to move to the **Quit screen** – see **Quit** above.

Viewing images

Small versions of each image are shown in the Resource Gallery. Click and drag the slider on the slide bar to scroll through the images in the Resource Gallery, or click on the arrows to move the images frame by frame. Roll the pointer over an image to see the caption.

▶ Click on an image to view the screen-sized version of it.
▶ To return to the Resource Gallery click on **Back to Resource Gallery**.

Viewing videos

Click on the video icon of your choice in the Resource Gallery. In order to view the videos on this CD, you will need to have **QuickTime** installed on your computer (see 'Setting up your computer for optimal use' above).

Once at the video screen, use the buttons on the bottom of the video screen to operate the video. The slide bar can be used for a fast forward and rewind. To return to the Resource Gallery click on **Back to Resource Gallery**.

Listening to sound recordings

Click on the required sound icon. Use the buttons or the slide bar to hear the sound. A transcript will be displayed on the viewing screen where appropriate. To return to the Resource Gallery, click on **Back to Resource Gallery**.

Printing

Click on the image to view it (see 'Viewing images' above). There are two print options:

Print using Acrobat enables you to print a high-quality version of an image. Choosing this option means that the image will open as a read-only page in **Adobe Acrobat** and in order to access these files you will need to have already installed **Adobe Acrobat Reader** on your computer (see 'Setting up your computer for optimal use' above). To print the selected resource, select **File** and then **Print**. Once you have printed the resource **minimise** or **close** the Adobe screen using — or X in the top right-hand corner of the screen. Return to the Resource Gallery by clicking on **Back to Resource Gallery**.

Simple print enables you to print a lower quality version of the image without the need to use Adobe Acrobat Reader. Select the image and click on the **Simple print** option. After printing, click on **Back to Resource Gallery**.

Slideshow presentation

If you would like to present a number of resources without having to return to the Resource Gallery and select a new image each time, you can compile a slideshow. Click on the + tabs at the top of each image in the Resource Gallery you would like to include in your presentation (pictures, sound and video can be included). It is important that you click on the images in the order in which you would like to view them (a number will appear on each tab to confirm the order). If you would like to change the order, click on **Clear slideshow** and begin again.

Once you have selected your images – up to a maximum of 20 – click on **Play slideshow** and you will be presented with the first of your selected resources. To move to the next selection in your slideshow click on **Next slide**, to see a previous resource click on **Previous slide**. You can end your slideshow presentation at any time by clicking on **Resource Gallery**. Your slideshow selection will remain selected until you **Clear slideshow** or return to the **Menu screen**.

Viewing on an interactive whiteboard or data projector

Resources can be viewed directly from the CD. To make viewing easier for a whole class, use a large monitor, data projector or interactive whiteboard. For group, paired or individual work, the resources can be viewed from the computer screen.

Photocopiable resources (PDF format)

To view or print a photocopiable resource page, click on the required title in the list and the page will open as a read-only page in **Adobe Acrobat**. In order to access these files you will need to have already installed **Adobe Acrobat Reader** on your computer (see 'Setting up your computer for optimal use' above). To print the selected resource select **File** and then **Print**. Once you have printed the resource **minimise** or **close** the Adobe screen using — or X in the top right-hand corner of the screen. This will take you back to the list of PDF files. To return to the **Menu screen**, click on **Back**.

BARNABY BEAR'S LOCAL AREA: CHESTER

Content and skills

This chapter links to unit 1, 'Around our school – the local area', and unit 5, 'Where in the world is Barnaby Bear?' of the QCA Scheme of Work for geography at Key Stage 1. The Resource Gallery for 'Barnaby Bear's local area: Chester' on the CD-ROM, together with the teacher's notes and photocopiable pages in this chapter, can be used when teaching these units.

As with the QCA Scheme of Work, this chapter encourages children to think about their own locality. It also develops their knowledge and understanding of the contrasting locality of Chester. The National Curriculum recognises that studying the local area is the most meaningful and accessible context for young children when beginning to develop geographical ideas and skills. Exploring Barnaby Bear's home locality of Chester will help children to understand how to study their own locality.

The teacher's notes contain background information about the resources and include ways of using them as a whole class, for group work or as individuals. Some of the activities link with other areas of the curriculum, such as literacy and ICT. Wherever possible, the activities encourage the children to ask questions and develop an enquiring approach to their learning.

© Chester City Council

Resources on the CD-ROM

The resources include images of specific locations around Chester, as well as a variety of maps to develop the children's geographical understanding and skills. Barnaby Bear's home and school are also in the resources, so that the children can compare their own locality to Barnaby's. Together, these resources provide a focused locality study of Chester and this approach can be mirrored to build a resource gallery of the children's own locality.

Photocopiable pages

The photocopiable pages in the book are also provided in PDF format on the CD-ROM and can be printed from there. They include:
▶ word cards containing essential vocabulary for the unit
▶ a quiz on Chester, which involves the use of maps
▶ a study of the River Dee and the use of land around it
▶ an activity sheet on local shops
▶ a comparison of Chester's bridges
▶ an activity sheet on the Old Dee Bridge.

Geographical skills

This chapter identifies opportunities for developing specific geographical skills, including the use of geographical vocabulary, fieldwork skills, using maps and plans and utilising secondary sources, such as asking and answering geographical questions.

NOTES ON THE CD-ROM RESOURCES

Chester in the British Isles

Great Britain is the largest island in Europe and includes Scotland, England, Wales and adjacent islands. It does not include the Channel Islands or the Isle of Man. These islands are not part of Great Britain or the United Kingdom as they are self-governing British Crown Dependencies.

The United Kingdom is made up of England, Scotland, Wales and Northern Ireland. It was officially created in 1921 after the constitution of the Irish Free State (now the Republic of Ireland). The United Kingdom describes a political union and is classed as a country.

The British Isles is a geographical rather than a political term. It refers to a group of islands in north-west Europe. The countries of the British Isles include the United Kingdom and the Republic of Ireland. The two largest islands of the British Isles are Ireland and Great Britain.

Chester is located within the British Isles, Great Britain and, therefore, the United Kingdom. Expecting young children to understand and remember the differences between these terms is ambitious, but still worth introducing at this stage as misconceptions are common later on. It is also important that children have the opportunity to locate the area of study at the beginning of each new unit. This will help them to develop a locational framework – that is, an understanding of where places are in relation to each other.

Discussing the map

▶ Ask the children if they know what a map is and what it can be used for. Explain that the whole geographical area they can see is called the British Isles.

▶ Indicate where land and sea are located on the map.

▶ Read the different parts of the United Kingdom with the children: Scotland, England, Wales and Northern Ireland. Explain that the United Kingdom is a country.

▶ Ask the children if they can find their locality on the map.

▶ Point out the location of Chester and ask the children to identify which part of the United Kingdom it is in (north-west England).

▶ Explain that a famous bear called Barnaby lives in Chester and that this is his local area.

Activities

▶ Help the children to locate the British Isles on a simple world map.

▶ Explain that Barnaby Bear really enjoys travelling around the world and display a world map in the classroom. Indicate on it any places visited by Barnaby through the geography curriculum, including the locality of the school.

▶ Ask the children to think about the sorts of activities Barnaby might do in Chester. For example, visit the library or go to school. Then ask the children to think about the activities that they do in their own locality.

▶ Use the 'Map word cards' on photocopiable page 17 with the children, as appropriate.

Street map of Chester

Chester is an historic settlement and originated as a Roman legionary fortress called Deva almost 2000 years ago. Originally a fortress and port, the site was ideal for defensive purposes, being a flat-topped hill on a river bend. The function of the settlement of Chester has evolved from being a defensive site in early Roman times and a major port in medieval times, to being a tourism and commercial centre today. Much has been retained from the past and Chester is well known for its heritage.

This simplified street map shows the location of many of the photographs included in this chapter. The list of key features includes: the City Walls, the Eastgate Clock, the River Dee, the Groves, The Rows, Handbridge, Westminster Park (arrow to), the Greyhound Retail Park, the Roodee railway viaduct and the bridges.

Discussing the map

▶ Ask the children what they think this map can be used for. Explain that this map has been produced for use by people visiting Chester (tourists).

▶ Ask the children to identify some of the features on the map if they can, such as the river, a bridge, a road.

▶ Identify and locate some of the key features, as listed above.
▶ Look together at the key. Challenge the children to find the symbols on the map and discuss what they mean.

Activities
▶ Using only the information on the map, discuss briefly with the children what they think Chester will be like. Produce a mind map of ideas.
▶ Ask the children to list any questions they would like to ask Barnaby about Chester. Children could go online in small groups and send their questions to Barnaby directly (www.bbc.co.uk/schools/barnabybear/). Explain to the children that their lists of questions and initial ideas will be reviewed at the end of the unit.
▶ Let the children complete the photocopiable 'Chester quiz' on page 21. In doing this, they will be exploring the location and position of some of the key features on the map.
▶ Show the children some of the photographs of Chester on the CD, such as 'The Walls and Eastgate clock' or 'The Rows' and ask the children to find them on the map. Explain that each of the photographs will be discussed in more detail during subsequent lessons.

OS map of Chester

This is an OS map of Chester at 1:25 000 scale. It is important to expose children to maps that they are likely to use in the future, even at this early stage. Key aspects of mapping which could be developed using Ordnance Survey maps include:
Distance – children could use string to work out longest and shortest routes.
Direction – children could follow a route on the map and give simple directions (left, right...).
Position – children could identify features on a map (next to, behind, in front of...).
Representation – recognising Ordnance Survey symbols.
Perspective – recognising a map as a bird's eye view and that things look different from above.

Discussing the map
▶ Explain to the children that this is a map of Chester. Explain that Ordnance Survey maps show a lot more detail than street maps and are designed to help people in finding their way to, from and around different places.
▶ Point out the scale. Explain that the largest scale is life-sized and that maps show things at a smaller scale. Explain to the children that the vertical grid lines point north on OS maps.
▶ Ask the children if they can see any of the features they may have previously identified, such as the City Walls, the River Dee. What additional features are shown?

Activities
▶ Compare this map with the 'Street map of Chester' (provided on the CD). Explain that the OS map shows a lot more of the area around Chester.
▶ As a class, compare this map with an Ordnance Survey map of the children's locality (preferably at the same scale). Which features and/or symbols are common to both localities? What are the main differences?
▶ Ask the children to develop their own local area map with symbols and a key.

The Walls and Eastgate Clock

The City Walls at Chester offer a complete 3km circuit around the city centre. The earliest defences were established by the Romans around the legionary fortress of Deva. These defences comprised four gates and simple street patterns within the rectangle. The Saxons then extended the Walls to create a fortified town. Only small sections of the Walls exist today.
   The Eastgate Clock is the most photographed clock in England after Big Ben. It is situated on the east side of the Walls at Eastgate. It was built to commemorate Queen Victoria's Diamond Jubilee of 1897, but was actually set to start on Queen Victoria's 80th birthday on 24 May, 1899. Originally wound each week, the whole mechanism is now electrically operated.

Discussing the photograph
▶ Ask the children what they can see in the photograph.
▶ Point out the tall buildings and note the number of storeys. Explain that these tend to be built within city centres where space is limited.

▶ Talk about the bridge. Explain that this is the Eastgate of the defensive City Walls.
▶ Discuss the ornate Eastgate Clock. Ask the children what time is shown (3.55pm) and who might be using the city centre at this time on a weekday (tourists, young families, retired people).

Activities
▶ Ask the children to consider why people might visit their locality and to list features which might interest tourists.
▶ Distribute photographs taken of attractions in your locality to small groups of children. Ask each group to find out about and produce a page on the feature shown in their picture. Collate all pages to produce a class guide to the local area for tourists.
▶ Show the children other photographs of Chester, such as the 'River Dee' provided on the CD) and let them use the information to design posters to encourage tourists to visit Chester.

Barnaby Bear's house

This is the 'home' of the fictional character Barnaby Bear. It is a semi-detached building which was probably built in the 1930s.

There is tremendous diversity in the range of buildings and homes within Chester. Barnaby's home is situated outside the city walls within a suburb where building space is less restricted and where more semi-detached and detached properties are typically found. Because Chester was built as a defensive site, it has restricted space for building within its centre.

Discussing the picture
▶ Ask the children what sort of house Barnaby Bear lives in. Talk about the term 'semi-detached' and discuss what it means.
▶ Discuss the sorts of homes the children live in and ask if anyone lives in a house like Barnaby's (be sensitive to the backgrounds and home situations of the children in your class).
▶ Talk about where they think Barnaby's house might be located and why. Explain that a suburb is a residential area outside the city centre.

Activities
▶ Using the 'OS map of Chester' (provided on the CD), ask the children to find where they think Barnaby Bear's house might be located and why. Note the names of suburbs on the map, such as Handbridge and Queen's Park, and explain that these are predominantly residential estates where bigger houses with gardens tend to be found.
▶ The children could go online and ask questions to Barnaby about his home (www. bbc.co.uk/schools/barnabybear/). For example, Do you have a back garden to play in? They could then use the responses or their imagination to produce some work about Barnaby's home. For example, they could draw a simple map of each floor with a key to show how each room is used.
▶ Looking at online estate agents' details of houses for sale in Chester and in the local area, get the children to compare building types. Can they identify simple patterns? For example, in Chester, flats and tall townhouses tend to be found within the city centre, whereas semi-detached and detached properties with gardens tend to be located outside the City Walls. Are similar patterns found within the children's local area?

River Dee

This image shows a view of the River Dee. Its source is in the mountains of the Snowdonia National Park in North Wales and is located to the west of Bala Lake (Llyn Tegid). At this point the river is known as Afon Dyindwy, or the Little Dee.

The Romans originally named the fortress of Chester Deva (meaning Divine or Goddess) and this referred to the great river which flowed just outside the City Walls. From Roman times, the River Dee was a great shipping river before developing into a significant port area during the 13th century. However, over time, the River Dee began to silt up and this led to the rise of the port at Liverpool and to changes in land use on the River Dee.

The area shown in the photograph is known as The Groves, Chester's riverfront, which was first established during the 18th century. There are a variety of features, which can be seen here, including public houses, cafes, paintings for sale, a 19th-century bandstand and landing stages where rowing and motorboats can be hired.

Discussing the photograph

▶ Discuss the things the children can see in the photograph and help them to define which are physical and which are human features. Discuss how the two types of features relate to each other. For example, residents are able to hire leisure boats because they live near to a river.

▶ Ask the children to mind map what they know about rivers. Have they ever seen one, visited or travelled on one?

▶ Explain that the river in the photograph is called the River Dee. Is there a river close to the school? What is it called?

▶ Explain that Barnaby Bear likes to travel on the rowing boats on the River Dee. Ask the children to describe what he might see as he travels along The Groves and explain that this is the name of the area at the riverfront.

Activities

▶ Using a simple map of the UK, show the children where the River Dee begins and ends.

▶ Look at the 'Street map of Chester' (provided on the CD) with the children. Can they find The Groves area on this map? Note that it is on the south side of the City, next to the River Dee. Ask the children to colour The Groves area and the river on a printout of the map.

▶ Produce a class display of The Groves area, showing Barnaby Bear travelling down the river. Use the maps to identify and label the features that he will see on his journey.

The Rows

The Rows in Chester are quite unique with their tiers of shops that line parts of the four main streets of Chester: Eastgate Street, Northgate Street, Watergate Street and Bridge Street. Each of these four streets lead down to the four gates, all of which featured as part of the original Roman fortress built 2000 years ago.

There are many theories relating to the construction of The Rows. A popular theory is that many of The Rows date from the end of the 13th century. Traditionally, The Rows had stone undercrofts at ground-floor level. These were not built below the ground because of the nature of the bedrock. The undercrofts were traditionally used as shops and warehouses. In the photograph, the undercrofts are now used as shops. Above the undercroft were living quarters which may have had shops at the front. Finally, on the top floor, the black and white architecture of what would have been the private chambers can be seen. Today some of these are used as a third or even a fourth shopping level, while others are still private or business accommodation.

Discussing the photograph

▶ Point out to the children what would have been the undercrofts, the living quarters (or halls) and the private chambers in the past. Explain that these have different uses today.

▶ Ask the children what type of building they would find in the centre of their settlement and compare this with Chester.

▶ Ask the children to guess what time of year this photograph was taken. Challenge any stereotypes about weather conditions across the different seasons. For example, statistically rainfall is equally likely to occur within any season.

Activities

▶ Using the 'Street map of Chester' (provided on the CD), help the children to locate the central shopping area (The Rows), which lines parts of the four main streets.

▶ Look at pictures of the centre of the children's locality and ask the children to compare building and shop types with those in Chester.

▶ Find out more about the old buildings of Chester by visiting the Chester City Council Tourism website at www.cccouncil.gov.uk

Deeside Court

This new development (the furthest right of the buildings), close to the city centre, has been built on the site of a former government office building. The development comprises two blocks. The north block contains four flats, while the south block (shown in the photograph) contains 14. The development was completed in September 2004 and the first residents moved in on 2 October. The flats have been designed with mature couples in mind, who perhaps do not have children. The flats are relatively large as they are an alternative to a detached home.

This is an interesting development as Dee Hills Park is a conservation area. The main challenges facing the developers were to ensure that the size and scale of the development was in keeping with neighbouring buildings. The scheme is unusual, not only because planning permission was granted within a conservation area, but also because it is the only modern apartment development in Chester where the residents have mooring rights on the river.

Discussing the photograph
▶ Ask the children what they can see. Note the river and two buildings – one large, older building with turrets and one large, modern-looking building (Deeside Court).
▶ Explain the differences between the two buildings (age) and the similarities (residential).
▶ Ask the children which building they prefer and which they would prefer to live in. Why?
▶ Do the children think Deeside Court should have been built here? What would Barnaby think about the new development?
▶ Can the children explain how this new building compares to the old buildings in the city centre, such as The Rows?

Activities
▶ Using the 'Street map of Chester' and the 'OS map of Chester' (provided on the CD), challenge the children to find the location of Dee Hills Park.
▶ Using the 'Building word cards' on photocopiable page 20, talk to the children about the type of home found in Deeside Court and other types of homes that they might live in.

Duke's Manor

This photograph is of Duke's Manor residential development in Chester. Compared with Deeside Court, it is slightly further from Chester city centre on a busy main road leading out of Chester (Liverpool Road). The estate comprises a range of houses, and the target market is young people.

The development is within walking distance of the city centre, and has excellent gymnasiums, swimming pools, a large sports centre and supermarket within short walking distance. Compared with Deeside Court, it would be less expensive to rent or to buy a property here, although it is still a desirable location.

Discussing the photograph
▶ Ask the children to identify features of the buildings in Duke's Manor. They are very different to the buildings in the city centre.
▶ How do the houses in Duke's Manor compare to the children's own homes? Are there houses like these in their own locality?
▶ Explain that developments of this kind are now being blocked in Chester and Cheshire, as there is a fear that the character of the region may be affected by too many new developments.

Activities
▶ Look with the children at the photograph 'Deeside Court' (provided on the CD) and ask them to explain the main differences between the two developments.
▶ As a class, list the key attractions and features of the Deeside Court and Duke's Manor developments. Ask the children to record where they would prefer to live and why.
▶ Compare this photograph with that of 'Barnaby Bear's house' (provided on the CD), which is also situated outside the city centre. How are they the same? How are they different?

Barnaby Bear's school: play area, entrance, classroom

This series of three photographs shows different parts of Barnaby Bear's school in Chester. There are many schools in Chester and they tend to be situated outside the City Walls, close to the outlying residential areas or suburbs.

The first photograph shows the school grounds. In Barnaby's school, the children and staff take great pride in their landscaped school grounds. They believe that the grounds should represent a pleasant and pleasing environment, which blends in as far as possible with the natural landscape.

The second photograph shows the main entrance to Barnaby's school and the third photograph shows a classroom.

Discussing the photographs

▶ Ask the children to identify what they can see in the series of photographs.
▶ Focus on the first photograph and ask them to say what words come to mind, such as green or quiet. Ask the children to compare this photograph with their own school grounds.
▶ Focusing on the second photograph, ask the children whether they think this is an old or new building, and what it is made of.
▶ Focus on the third photograph and ask the children to list what they can see in this classroom, such as a globe, books, a computer and class displays. Do the children have a globe or a world map in their class too? Discuss how they can find out about different places around the world.

Activities

▶ Ask the children to draw a picture or a simple map to depict their school grounds.
▶ As a class, list some questions relating to the school building. For example, When was it built? What is it built from? Why was it built here? Ask the headteacher if there are any local residents (perhaps on the governing body) who could help them to find out the answers.
▶ In small groups, provide the children with a simple base plan of the classroom and some symbols in the form of a key to represent a computer, chairs, desks, and so on. Ask the children to cut out the symbols and produce a map of their classroom.

Local shops

This is a local parade of shops situated in one of the suburban areas of Chester. This residential estate is called Westminster Park and is located on the south side of the city. Barnaby Bear's teacher lives here and her name is Mrs Glass. Barnaby's school is also located here. There is a big park nearby and both the estate and the park are located outside the City Walls.

Discussing the photograph

▶ Explain to the children what the photograph shows. Also mention that Barnaby Bear's school is located here.
▶ Ask the children to list the types of shops they can see. Ask why these shops are located here and who they may serve. Explain that they are convenience stores for local residents.
▶ Ask the children where they go shopping in the local area. Do they have convenience stores close by? If so, what types of shops are they? Are they similar to those in Westminster Park?

Activities

▶ Ask the children to draw a simple plan of the shops at Westminster Park using representative symbols and a key. For example, fruit for the greengrocer, a knife and fork for the Chinese takeaway. This activity can be used with the photocopiable 'Local shops' on page 23.
▶ Let the children write a shopping list for Barnaby Bear based on the shops in the photograph.
▶ Through fieldwork in the local area, the children could produce a 'photo map' of a parade of shops close to the school. They could photograph each shop front and display these on the classroom wall as a plan or map. They could also include symbols and a key.

Greyhound Retail Park

One of the main functions of Chester is retail and this economic activity continues to significantly boost the local economy. Retail provides around 20 per cent of jobs in the city and £500 million. Around six million visitors travel to Chester each year and spend money in the city's restaurants, hotels and shops. Around £350 million is generated through tourism each year.

There are a number of retail outlets in Chester, one of which is the Greyhound Retail Park. This is classified as an 'out of town' facility, which means that it is within one or two miles of the city centre. There are a number of major chain stores accommodated here.

Discussing the photograph

▶ Discuss with the children what can be seen in the photograph. Point out the flat land (the former flood plain of the River Dee), which is ideal for building a retail park.
▶ Discuss the size of the retail outlets compared with shops in the city centre or convenience stores. Point out how the size of the car parks relates to the size of the retail outlets.
▶ Discuss why retail parks attract so many shoppers: free parking, the range of outlets within one area.

Activities
▶ Display a map of the local area on the wall and identify where the children go shopping. If appropriate, group types of shops, such as those in a retail park, local convenience stores, central shops. Colour code the map and add a simple key.
▶ As a homework activity, ask the children to find out what sorts of products they/their parents buy from these sorts of shops. Add product lists and labels to the display. For example, a takeaway menu for the convenience stores, a DVD player from the retail park.

Roodee Racecourse
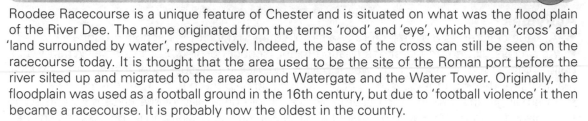

Roodee Racecourse is a unique feature of Chester and is situated on what was the flood plain of the River Dee. The name originated from the terms 'rood' and 'eye', which mean 'cross' and 'land surrounded by water', respectively. Indeed, the base of the cross can still be seen on the racecourse today. It is thought that the area used to be the site of the Roman port before the river silted up and migrated to the area around Watergate and the Water Tower. Originally, the floodplain was used as a football ground in the 16th century, but due to 'football violence' it then became a racecourse. It is probably now the oldest in the country.

Discussing the photograph
▶ Ask the children what they think the photograph shows. Point out the flatness of the land, the racing activity, the crowds and the large building in the distance.
▶ Ask the children what they think this area might be used for when the racing season is over. For example, car boot sales, as a fairground site, as a wedding venue.

Activities
▶ As a class, write to the tourist information office in Chester for details about other tourist attractions in the area.
▶ Ask the children which attraction they would like to visit if they went to Chester. Get them to plan their day and consider the following: the mode of transport they would use given the distance of their home from Chester, an itinerary for the day given the season of their visit.

Grosvenor Bridge

The Grosvenor Bridge was built with a view to improving communications between Chester and North Wales. The Earl of Grosvenor laid the foundation stone of the new bridge and donated a considerable sum to the building fund in 1827. It was designed by Thomas Harrison and opened by Princess Victoria in 1832. At 60m long it has the longest, single span, stone archway in England. It is built from sandstone quarried in Peckforton (south-east of Chester).
   The bridge accommodates three lanes of traffic. There are two lanes that go into the city, and one lane that goes out towards Wrexham in a southerly direction.

Discussing the photograph
▶ Ask the children to look closely at the image and to suggest what is on the bridge (traffic and pedestrians) and what is under it (the River Dee).
▶ Ask the children to describe the bridge and then to compare it with other bridges, either within their local area or that they have travelled across elsewhere.
▶ Ask the children why bridges are built. Explain that in this case the bridge links Chester city centre with outlying areas and North Wales, by providing the means to cross the River Dee.

Activities
See activities for 'Queen's Park Suspension Bridge'.

Old Dee Bridge

It is believed that the Old Dee Bridge dates back to Roman times, and certainly features in the Doomsday records as early as Anglo-Saxon times. In the past, the bridge was the main link between Chester and North Wales. This route provided a link for troops and supplies during times of war, and for trade.
   The bridge has been rebuilt several times due to erosion caused by flooding and high tides, and has thus gradually evolved to become a bridge made of stone rather than timber. Until tolls were

abolished in 1885, it cost 1d (equivalent to $\frac{1}{2}$p) to take a cow across and 9d (4p) for a horse and carriage. This bridge now accommodates single lane traffic managed by traffic lights.

Discussing the photograph

▶ Explain to the children that this bridge also links Chester city centre to outlying areas and to North Wales, but is much older than the Grosvenor Bridge as it dates back to Roman times.

▶ Explain that in the background, the suburban area called Handbridge can be seen. The children should be able to see a church and residential housing.

▶ Ask the children to describe the bridge and then to compare it with other bridges they know.

Activities

See activities for 'Queen's Park Suspension Bridge'.

Queen's Park Suspension Bridge

The iron suspension bridge known as the Queen's Park Suspension Bridge also crosses the River Dee and was originally opened in 1852. It was then re-built in 1923. The bridge links Chester city centre and The Groves area with the outlying residential area of Queen's Park. It is a footbridge and is a crossing point for pedestrians only.

Discussing the photograph

▶ Ask the children to look closely at the image and to tell you what is on the bridge (pedestrians only) and what is under it (the River Dee).

▶ Explain that from Chester city centre, the suburban area called Queen's Park can be reached via this crossing point. The side of the bridge shown is located in The Groves area which is very popular with tourists. Note that many of the people in the photograph will be visitors.

Activities

▶ Show the children the 'Street map of Chester' (provided on the CD). Can they find the three bridges on this map?

▶ Ask the children to count the river-crossing points on the street map. How many are there?

▶ Give the children a copy of 'Crossing the Old Dee Bridge' on photocopiable page 25. Ask the children to work out how much it cost to take cows and carriages over the bridge in the past.

▶ Get the children to compare the three bridges, noting the similarities and differences. For instance, the Queen's Park Suspension Bridge only serves pedestrians.

NOTES ON THE PHOTOCOPIABLE PAGES

Word cards
PAGES 17-20

These cards show key words that children will encounter when working on the unit:
▶ words relating to the map of the British Isles
▶ words to describe specific locations in Chester
▶ words that describe different types of buildings.
The Chester word cards support the specific study of Barnaby Bear's locality. Encourage the children to build their own word bank that refers to places specific to their area.

Activities

▶ Cut out the cards and laminate them. Use the 'Map word cards' and 'Building word cards' as often as possible when talking about the British Isles, maps and buildings.

▶ Encourage the children to match the word cards to the pictures in the Resource Gallery.

▶ Use the 'Building word cards' for displays about homes and houses.

Chester quiz
PAGE 21

Use this quiz in conjunction with the 'Street map of Chester' (provided on the CD) to develop the children's map reading skills and also help to show them why maps are useful. Encourage the children to use positional language (top, bottom, left, right) and direction terms (north, south, east and west) when describing where symbols and places are on the map.

Activities
▶ For less able children, read the questions out loud and encourage them to look for the symbols on the map.
▶ More able children can work in groups and one child can be appointed 'quiz master'. Ask them to give reasons why they chose to circle particular symbols.
▶ Develop the quiz with further enquiry questions, such as, Where is the best car park for shopping? How do you get to Northgate Arena from the closest car park?

The River Dee
PAGE 22

This illustration is a representation of the types of tourist attractions that children may see on the riverside in Chester, particularly in The Groves area. It shows paintings for sale on the steps, a restaurant (with outdoor seating in sunny weather), an ice-cream parlour and van, a cafe, public toilets, a coach (possibly for tourists), different types of boating and a river cruise boat.

Activities
▶ Print out the picture and place it in the middle of a board or large sheet of paper. Help the children use the appropriate 'Chester word cards' (on photocopiable page 19) to label the picture and ask them to name the features in the picture.
▶ Give each child a copy of the photocopiable sheet and ask groups to colour the picture in to represent spring, summer and autumn (green leaves in spring, brown leaves in autumn). Ask them why this scene would be very different in winter.

Local shops
PAGE 23

This activity sheet encourages the children to think about the use of symbols. Explain to the children that the symbols are a clear and simple way to show what a feature or building is on a map. Some shops have signs hanging outside to show what they sell. Explain that this is helpful if someone doesn't know the language in a country – they would know what the shop sold even if they couldn't read the sign.

Activities
▶ Talk through the shops listed with the children. Ask them what symbol would best represent each shop, and why, before they draw their symbols.
▶ Take a photograph of shops in the local area. Ask the children to draw signs and stick them around the picture.

Chester's bridges
PAGE 24

Use this activity sheet after discussing the pictures of Chester's bridges in the Resource Gallery. Encourage the children to describe the bridges. How are they similar and different? Let them use the drawing frame to record their observations.

Crossing the Old Dee Bridge
PAGE 25

During Victorian times (until 1885), people had to pay a toll to cross the Old Dee Bridge. It used to cost 1d (equivalent to $\frac{1}{2}$p today), to take a cow across. Therefore, to take two cows across would be the equivalent today of 1p. A horse and carriage cost 9d (approximately 4p today).

Activities
▶ Make a number of copies of the photocopiable sheet and cut out the cards. Begin by asking the children to pair a picture of two cows with a picture of 1p. Then develop the game by mixing the cards and asking how much it would cost, for example, to take four cows and a horse and carriage across the bridge.
▶ For more able children, reverse the game by asking what they could take across if they only had a certain amount of money.

Great Britain

island

country

United Kingdom

British Isles

Chester

The City Walls

The Eastgate Clock

The River Dee

The Groves

The Rows

Handbridge

Westminster Park

Greyhound Retail Park

railway viaduct

Old Dee Bridge

Grosvenor Bridge

Queen's Park Suspension Bridge

semi-detached

detached

flat

terraced

suburb

city centre

Chester quiz

Barnaby and his parents are going shopping in Chester. They are going to drive there.

- Find the car parks **P**. How many can you see?

_____

- Circle the best car park for Barnaby and his parents to park in.

Northgate Arena has a very big swimming pool. Barnaby is going to have his first swimming lesson on Saturday.

- Describe where Northgate Arena is.

_____

_____

- Circle the nearest car park **P**.

Barnaby will be travelling by train to visit his friend in Manchester on Sunday.

- Circle the railway station **≷**.

Barnaby wants to find out more about his town.

- Circle the Tourist Information Offices **i**.

SCHOLASTIC PHOTOCOPIABLE

Local shops

- Draw your own signs for these shops.

general store	Chinese take-away
bakery	**greengrocer**
wine shop	**kitchen shop**

Chester's bridges

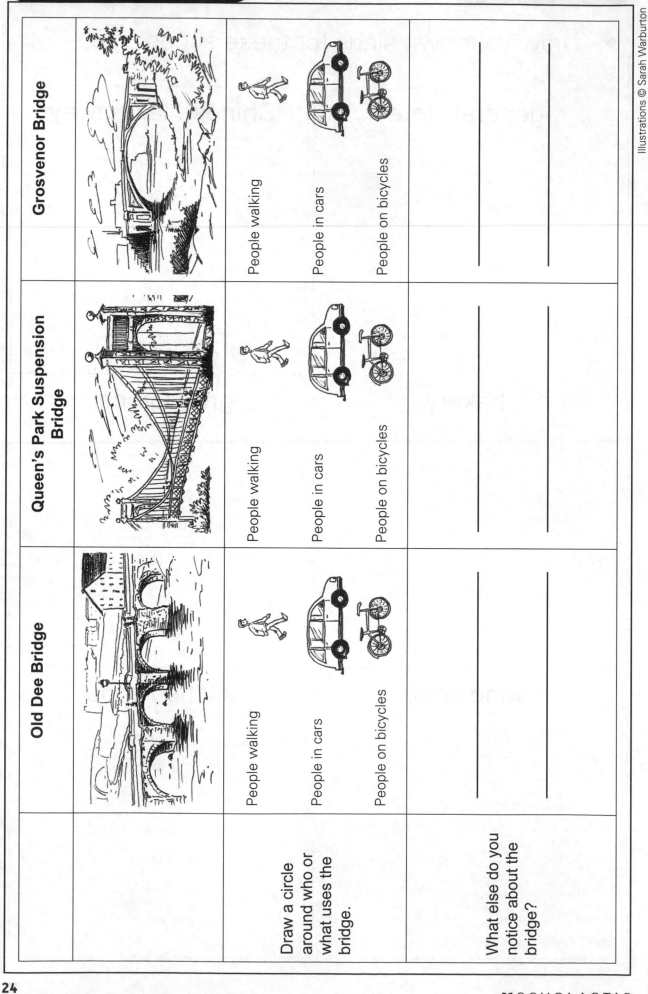

	Grosvenor Bridge	Queen's Park Suspension Bridge	Old Dee Bridge
Draw a circle around who or what uses the bridge.	People walking People in cars People on bicycles	People walking People in cars People on bicycles	People walking People in cars People on bicycles
What else do you notice about the bridge?			

Illustrations © Sarah Warburton

■SCHOLASTIC
PHOTOCOPIABLE

Crossing the Old Dee Bridge

- This is how much it used to cost to cross the Old Dee Bridge.
  - 2 cows = 1p
  - 1 horse and carriage = 4p

British coins by courtesy of The Royal Mint © Crown Copyright. Illustrations © Sarah Warburton

AN ISLAND HOME: COLL

Content and skills

This chapter links to unit 3, 'An island home,' of the QCA Scheme of Work for geography at Key Stage 1. The Resource Gallery for 'An island home: Coll' on the CD-ROM, together with the teacher's notes and photocopiable pages in this chapter, can be used to support this unit.

This chapter focuses on the Isle of Coll, on which the fictional Isle of Struay in the Katie Morag books is based. The resources help to develop the children's knowledge and understanding of an island home, both real and fictional. This section also works as a contrasting locality study for the children.

The teacher's notes contain background information about the resources and include ways of using them as a whole class, for group work or as individuals. Some of the activities link with other areas of the curriculum, such as literacy and ICT. Wherever possible, the activities encourage the children to ask questions and develop an enquiring approach to their learning.

Resources on the CD-ROM

The resources include photographs that illustrate all aspects of an island home: transport, people, buildings and landscapes. A variety of maps at different scales show different aspects of Coll and the contrasting mainland town of Oban. Audio clips of Hebridean music and environmental sounds add another dimension to the study of an island home. There is also a short film of a ferry arriving at Coll. Katie Morag's family tree and a map of the Isle of Struay are provided on the CD-ROM and they act as a starting point for the study of the real Isle of Coll.

Photocopiable pages

The photocopiable pages in the book are also provided in PDF format on the CD-ROM, from which they can be printed. They include:
▶ word cards containing essential vocabulary for the unit
▶ an activity sheet on map symbols
▶ a worksheet on time and travelling to Coll
▶ a writing frame to investigate the features of an island
▶ profiles of Mairi Hedderwick and other people from Coll.

Geographical skills

This chapter identifies opportunities for developing specific geographical skills, including the use of geographical vocabulary, fieldwork skills and the use of maps and plans. It also develops the use of secondary sources, in asking and answering geographical questions.

NOTES ON THE CD-ROM RESOURCES

Isle of Struay

This is a map of Struay, the fictional island on which the stories of Katie Morag are based. The author, Mairi Hedderwick, based the background for her series on the Isle of Coll – a small island situated within the Inner Hebrides. Many comparisons can be drawn between the Isles of Struay and Coll: small islands, the port and bay areas, a low population density, farming as a significant economic activity, lighthouses on cliffs, lochs and inland water features, a castle (there are two on Coll) and that both islands contain only one general shop and a post office.

Discussing the map

▶ Show the children the map and explain that the Isle of Struay is a fictional version of the Isle of Coll.
▶ Point out some of the key features identified above, so that when Coll is introduced the children are prepared to draw comparisons.

Activities

▶ As a class, make a list of key features on the map and save this as a class document (electronic or otherwise) for use when Coll is introduced.
▶ Introduce an additional column next to the list of features. Tick those features the children suggest can be found in the local area, or which the children feel knowledgeable about, and put a question mark beside those features that the children need to find out more about.
▶ Use the 'Mairi Hedderwick' sheet on photocopiable page 46 to tell the story of Mairi Hedderwick in small groups.
▶ Tell the story *Katie Morag Delivers the Mail.* Display the map for the class to see. Ask the children to identify the route taken by Katie Morag as she delivers the mail. What features does Katie pass? Did Katie take the shortest route?
▶ In small groups, the children could write their own story about the Isle of Struay, using the 'Isle of Struay word cards' on photocopiable page 42 as a starting point.
▶ Let the children produce their own map of an imaginary island they would like to live on.

Katie Morag's family tree

This is Katie Morag's family tree, produced by the author of the Katie Morag series, Mairi Hedderwick. Katie Morag is actually based on what Mairi always wanted to be – apparently she had always wanted red hair as a child!

Discussing the picture

▶ Explain to the children that this picture is called a family tree and it shows members of Katie Morag's family.
▶ Talk about why it is called a family tree. Point out how the people are linked, with all the lines looking like branches.
▶ If the children are familiar with the Katie Morag stories, ask them to identify the family members.
▶ Ask the children to suggest which of the occupations featured within the Katie Morag series they think would be undertaken on the Isle of Coll today.

Activities

▶ Ask the children to produce their own family tree for their immediate family (and grandparents), finding out what jobs people do now and in the past. They could be encouraged to make displays with real photographs or draw the pictures like Katie Morag's.
▶ Help the children find out about the range of jobs people do in the local area. Relate this to its human and physical geography. For example, working at a ferry terminal if the locality is coastal.

British Isles map

Great Britain is the largest island in Europe and includes Scotland, England, Wales and adjacent islands. It does not include the Channel Islands (which include Jersey and Guernsey) or the Isle of Man. These islands are self-governing British Crown Dependencies.

The United Kingdom is made up of England, Scotland, Wales and Northern Ireland. It officially came into being in 1922 after the constitution of the Irish Free State (now the Republic of Ireland). The United Kingdom describes a political union and is classed as a country.

The British Isles is a geographical rather than a political term. It refers to a group of Islands in north-west Europe. The countries of the British Isles include the UK and the Republic of Ireland. The two largest islands of the British Isles are Ireland and Great Britain. The British Isles also includes Orkney and the Shetland Islands, Inner and Outer Hebrides, the Isle of Man, the Isle of Wight, the Channel Islands and other small islands.

Coll is located within the Inner Hebrides of Scotland, the British Isles, Great Britain and, therefore, the United Kingdom.

Expecting young children to understand and remember the differences between these terms is ambitious but still worth introducing at this stage as misconceptions are common later on. It is also important that children have the opportunity to locate the area of study at the beginning of each new unit. This will help them to develop a locational framework – an understanding of where places are in relation to each other.

Discussing the map

▶ Ask the children if they know what a map is and what it can be used for. Explain that the whole geographical area shown is called the British Isles.

▶ Indicate where land and sea are located on the map.

▶ Ask the children if they can name the different parts of the United Kingdom. Explain that the United Kingdom is a country.

▶ Can the children approximate the location of their settlement on the map?

▶ Point out the location of Coll and ask the children to identify which part of the United Kingdom it is in (off the west coast of Scotland). Explain that Coll is an island. Reiterate that the fictional Isle of Struay is based on the real Isle of Coll.

Activities

▶ Let the children locate the British Isles on a simple world map.

▶ Ask the children to bring in a photograph of themselves taken anywhere in the world (preferably when on holiday). Add photographs and locations to a world map display. Has anyone visited a small island? Has anyone visited Scotland or the Inner/Outer Hebrides?

OS map of Coll

This is an enlargement of an OS map of Coll from 1:250 000 scale. It is important to expose children to maps that they are likely to use in the future, even at this early stage. At Key Stages 2 and 3, children will be expected to be able to use Ordnance Survey maps, and of course, in adulthood, they are likely to use them frequently for navigation. For more information on using Ordnance Survey maps, see page 9.

Discussing the map

▶ Explain that this is a map of the Isle of Coll. Explain that Ordnance Survey maps show a lot of detail and are designed to help people in finding their way to, from and around different places.

▶ Explain that maps show things at a smaller scale and that everything shown on a map is usually much larger in reality.

Activities

▶ Using the 'Map symbols' sheet on photocopiable page 43, ask the children to draw the symbols and find them on the map.

▶ Let the children compare this map with an OS map of their locality (preferably at the same scale). Which features/symbols are common to both areas? What are the main differences? What do they notice about the size of the island compared with their home locality?

▶ Using an OS map, show the children places that could be travelled to in their locality in 45 minutes. Emphasise that this journey represents the entire length of the Isle of Coll.

Aerial view of Coll

This is an aerial image of Coll. The derivation for the name of Coll is not known, but it would seem to be pre-Norse as it is referred to in Adomnán's *Life of Columba*. In the older references it appears as 'Cholla' or 'Kolli'. The Vikings were raiding in Hebridean waters by the 8th century and soon afterwards they were establishing settlements on the islands. Coll was a place of some importance during the Norse occupations and it is mentioned in *Njal's Saga* as the headquarters of Earl Gilli, representative and brother-in-law of Sigurd, who ruled the Orkneys and Hebrides about AD1000. See the history section of the Coll website for more information on the history of Coll and early settlers (www.isleofcoll.org/history).

In 2004 the island had 160 inhabitants, 25 of whom were children. The island has about 90 homes and some of these are holiday homes. The main settlement is the village of Arinagour where most people live. The remaining population live in groups of two to three houses or farms scattered across the island. There are also two large, inhabited castles on the island.

The present day economy of the island is based on tourism, building construction, the Project Trust gap-year organisation (the island's biggest employer), farming, fishing, the RSPB reserve and IT employment. Only 11 per cent of the economy is agricultural and the farming does not include dairy cows.

Discussing the photograph

▶ Explain to the children that this is a photograph of the island from above, rather than a drawing or map. Why do they think the island might be described as 'fish-shaped'?
▶ What can the children see in the photograph? Are there any clues as to what the land is like on Coll? Point out features such as the beaches, fields and hills.

Activities

▶ Compare this view with the 'OS map of Coll' and the 'Simple map of Coll' (provided on the CD). These are all different views of the island but can the children spot any similarities? How do the different views match up?
▶ Use an oblique aerial view of the children's own locality to talk about how places look very different from the air. Although this photograph of Coll is taken from very far away, it's still clear that there are not a lot of settlements on the island.

Simple map of Coll

This is a simple map of Coll, which has been specifically produced for use by Key Stage 1 children by Wildgoose Education Resources. Some important features have been labelled. For example, Loch na Cloiche. This feature has a 'crannog', an artificial island constructed by past dwellers, usually to protect them from marauders. Ben Hogh is the highest point at 106m and offers a fantastic panoramic view. There is an interesting 'erratic' situated here (a big boulder), perched on three smaller boulders. It almost looks as if human activity has positioned the boulders. Port Arinagour, as the main settlement, has been identified. This has been a sheltering harbour and port for a very long time, where boats call in to serve the population.

The island is low and rocky on the east side and is characterised by lots of bogs and small lochs. It has more varied features to the west, with grassy pasture, some bigger lochs, low bogs and heathery low-lying hills.

There is a bird sanctuary on the island. This wildlife and sea-life such as basking sharks and whales attract eco-tourists – visitors who travel to the island to observe the marine species, as well as to enjoy the intrinsic beauty of the landscape.

Sea fishing also brings significant economic benefit, even if it is only carried out regularly by about three men. Many people make a part-time living from tourism, usually by running a B&B or guest house. Some of these activities have the added benefit of providing local employment. This also applies to the one general shop, as well as the restaurant and the hotel. Several people are engaged in arts and crafts, including Tamara Hedderwick, who runs the pottery. Caledonian MacBrayne (the ferry company) and Argyll and Bute Council also provide several jobs.

Ewan and Sam's home is marked on the map as they are Tamara Hedderwick's sons. Both Sam and Ewan attend the primary school in Arinagour.

Discussing the map

▶ Ask the children to identify land and sea and reiterate that Coll is an island.
▶ Identify the main features using the simple key and explain what the features are.
▶ Talk about the different animals that are on the map. Can the children recognise them? What do they think these symbols mean? (Indications of the type of farming.)
▶ Point out the scale to the children and explain what it means.

Activities
▶ Use a map of the children's locality and trace the outline of the map of Coll onto it. Ask a child to cut around the outline. This will show the size of Coll in relation to an area that the children know well.
▶ How many of the symbols on the map would apply to the area around the school? Undertake some simple fieldwork in the local area, having produced a simple base map of the route to be taken. On this base map, 'hot spots' could be identified where children need to note what they see.
▶ On return to the classroom, the children could consider appropriate symbols and produce a simple map for the local area. Discuss any symbols and features which are common to both Coll and the school locality, and also identify differences based on field data and prior knowledge.

Beach on Coll

This photograph was probably taken at Feall Bay. Tourists like to visit the beaches around Coll and are particularly interested in bird watching and spotting other forms of wildlife, such as basking sharks, porpoises, dolphins, humpback whales and seals. Visitors like to walk around the sandy bays. Alternatively, there is a taxi service which does guided tours for tourists!

The micro-climate at Feall Bay is characterised by coastal breezes of varying wind direction. The northerly winds are much colder. In some spots it can be warmer and more sheltered.

There is a wide range of coastal plants and flowers within the sandy bays across the island. This includes some rare species, such as orchids, including the very rare Irish Ladies Tresses. During the summer, the beaches are characterised by beautiful carpets of flowers. In 2005, a book about the plants and flowers of Coll is being written and produced by the islanders.

Discussing the photograph
▶ Ask the children what they can see in the photograph and explain where it is. Also explain that tourists like to visit for other reasons than sunbathing (see above).
▶ Would the children like to visit this place? What might they do when they got there?

Activities
▶ Help the children to locate Feall Bay on the 'OS map of Coll' and the 'Simple map of Coll'. Then look together at the PDF of the 'Aerial view of Coll' and zoom in to find Feall Bay. Ask the children to describe how it looks from the air.
▶ Distribute holiday brochures (on coastal resorts) between small groups of children. Ask them to identify different activities, such as fishing, boating, sunbathing. Explain how different resorts offer different types of tourist activities, depending on where in the world they are and the main features that characterise them. Cut out relevant images and display on a world map.
▶ Compare this photograph to those in the 'Going to the Seaside' Resource Gallery to see how a beach on Coll compares to a beach at Tenby.

Coll inland

This photograph was taken at the west end of Coll, between the RSPB house and a working farm. Typical inland landscape can be seen here, characterised by low-lying machair and dune systems. The original bedrock of the island is called Lewisian Gneiss (pronounced 'nice') and is very, very old. It is thought that a fairly large ship was buried here in the past, by the sand dunes. The ship was reputably once exposed by a winter storm, but then covered up again.

Discussing the photograph
▶ What can the children see in the picture? Note the sheep in the foreground. Tell them that some of the land on Coll is used for farming.
▶ What human and physical features can the children see?
▶ Point out the stone walls and fences: they are two different types of enclosure. Which do the children think is more modern?
▶ How would the children describe the land? Would they want to go there?

Activities
▶ Compare the photograph with the resources in the 'Capitals' Resource Gallery. They all show different uses of land. What are the main differences between the uses of land?

▶ Give the children a copy of photocopiable page 45 to get them thinking about land use.
▶ Compare this image with the 'Aerial view of Coll'. Ask the children if they can tell where this photograph could have been taken. What are their reasons?

TRAVELLING TO AND AROUND COLL

OS map of Oban

One of the ways of getting to Coll from the mainland is to take a ferry from Oban. It is a busy port on the west coast of Scotland, with a population of about 8500 people. During the tourism season (May to October), Oban is a particularly busy port area with big ferry boats calling regularly, as well as fishing boats, yachts, tour boats and cruise boats.

As can be seen from the map, Oban is a large harbour with a pebbly foreshore and splendid views out to sea. These views can be seen most clearly from the small hill at the back of the town. The official Oban website (www.oban.ws) gives more information about the settlement.

Discussing the map
▶ Explain to the children that the map shows the Port of Oban on the Scottish mainland, and that it is from here that one can travel to Coll by ferry.
▶ Ask the children what they can see on the map. Point out the built-up areas, the sea, the harbour/bay, pebbly beaches, roads, boat trips, cycle hire and school.

Activities
See activities for 'OS map of Arinagour'.

OS map of Arinagour

This is a 1:25 000 scale OS map of Arinagour on the Isle of Coll. The ferries to and from Oban and the Isle of Tiree come here. Arinagour is a small village with few facilities, compared with Oban and other mainland settlements. There is one main street – a single-track road. There is no street furniture, such as street lights or traffic lights, and sheep wander freely across the road. There is a row of sea-facing cottages and 'Island Stores' (photograph provided on this CD) is the only shop on the island. Within the village there is one bistro-style restaurant, one hotel, a post office, a small petrol station and a fire station. Situated just outside the village is the old village hall and a new medical centre. Two hundred metres up the hill in the village is a small housing estate, which comprises 20 houses in a cul-de-sac and Arinagour primary school.

Discussing the map
▶ Explain to the children what the map shows and that they would arrive here if travelling from mainland Scotland or from neighbouring islands, such as Tiree.
▶ Ask the children what they can see on the map. Point out the sea, the harbour/bay, pebbly strips of beach (shingle), the sandy estuary, cliffs on the coastline, roads, boat trips, cycle hire and how the area isn't very built up.

Activities
▶ Let the children compare the 'OS map of Arinagour' with the 'OS map of Oban'. Which features/symbols are common to both areas (port or bay area, beaches, cycle hire, boat trips).
▶ What are the main differences between the two maps (Arinagour has fewer houses, is less built up, has no superstore, has sandy areas as well as pebble beaches, has a river estuary, some rocky areas and relief surrounding the port area).
▶ Referring to the 'British Isles map' (provided on the CD), explain how children at Arinagour primary school go on to secondary school in Oban. Indicate the route the children would take. Discuss how they would travel there and how long it would take.

Route map

This map shows the routes to Coll in simple form:
▶ Oban to Tiree to Coll.
▶ Glasgow to Tiree to Coll.

Caledonian MacBrayne is the name of the government-subsidised ferry company who service many of the Scottish Islands. There are six boats per week during the summer and three per week during the winter. It usually takes about three hours to travel from Oban to Coll.

Loganair Ltd (under a franchise partnership with British Airways) operate the flights from Glasgow to Tiree. This journey takes about 50 minutes. There is no airport on Coll, just an emergency landing strip (which is occasionally used by visiting private planes and helicopters) and a helicopter pad for the Air Ambulance.

There are other ways of travelling to Coll which are not shown on the map. Many people visit in their own yachts or sometimes their own charter flights.

Discussing the map

▶ Identify the routes on the map with the children.

▶ Explain to the children that flying from Glasgow to Oban can save time, as driving this distance would be a relatively long journey. Explain that tourists sometimes like to 'call' at Tiree on their way to Coll, as Tiree is a better-known tourist resort.

Activities

▶ Ask the children to predict which journey would take the longest. Then access the timetable and work out the time of each journey. Let the children note the times on a print out of the map.

▶ For homework, ask the children to find out about journeys they have taken (maybe on holiday or visiting someone) and modes of transport used. As a class, plot different routes taken by class members on a simple wipe on/wipe off world map. Use symbols to denote modes of transport. Discuss the range of journeys taken.

Mainland road

To get to Coll by ferry, people need to get to Oban first. This photograph was taken on the A85 towards Oban, in between Lochawe and Dalmally. The Southern Hills in the Grampian Mountains can be seen in the background. The route and width of roads built here will, to some extent, be determined by the physical geography of a mountainous region.

Discussing the photograph

▶ Explain to the children that this photograph was taken on the Scottish mainland, just a short distance from the port of Oban.

▶ Ask the children what they can see (a signpost with destinations and road numbers on), a two-lane road, mountains in the background).

Activities

▶ Tell the children to imagine that this is the view from their car window. Using the 'OS map of Oban' (provided on the CD), ask them to predict what they will see through the window when travelling through Oban to the point where they will catch the ferry to Coll.

▶ Make simple flashcards of different road signs and symbols the children might know, such as 'No entry' or a roundabout sign. Explain to the children that road signs and symbols help drivers to see quickly which way they need to go or what they need to be aware of ahead.

▶ Ask the children to identify points around the school building where a signpost would be useful for visitors. They can produce signs to indicate where key rooms or areas of the school are located. Encourage them to use directional language, such as left, right and straight on.

Coll road

The majority of the road network in Coll is single track, as shown in this photograph, due to the relatively low population density and the cost implications in terms of building and maintenance. There are numerous passing places, however, to allow cars to travel in both directions.

Flooding can be a problem in winter, and ice and snow also present problems. High winds and rain can make driving hazardous on occasion.

Discussing the photograph

▶ Ask the children what the picture shows. (A single-track road with open grasslands.)

▶ Do the children think that all the roads on Coll are like this? Explain that this is the case and ask the children for reasons why.

▶ Ask the children whether they have seen roads like this in their own locality and to identify other types of road they have travelled on.

Activities
▶ As a class, list differences between the road in this photograph and that featured in the 'Mainland road' photograph (provided on the CD). Make sure the children compare the single track road with the two-lane road and the uneven surface with the well-maintained one.
▶ Using the 'OS map of Coll' (provided on the CD), show the children how to use string and a scale to work out the length of the circuit of the road network on Coll. Compare this with a distance between two areas known to the children in their home region.

Ferry at Oban

This is the MV (Motor Vessel) *Clansman* at Oban. It can hold up to 90 cars and 638 passengers. Its sister ferry is the MV *Lord of the Isles*. It is a bit smaller and takes up to 56 cars and 506 passengers. They both connect the islands of the Inner Hebrides to Oban.

Discussing the photograph
▶ Ask the children to identify the features in the photograph.
▶ Explain that this is the pier at Oban, which is on the mainland of Scotland. This ferry takes people from the mainland to Coll and its neighbouring island Tiree.
▶ Point out the size of the ferry and ask the children to compare it to the size of the people and buildings nearby.
▶ Ask the children to imagine how big it is and tell them how many passengers and cars it can hold. Compare these numbers to the number of children in the school and number of cars in the school car park.

Activities
▶ Look together at the 'OS map of Oban' (provided on the CD). Point out where the ferry docks at Oban (the black line and arrow to the Quay). Point out the shaded areas that show where the land is built up – these are the buildings in the background of the photograph.
▶ Compare this photograph with that of 'Arinagour pier and ferry' (provided on the CD). Ask the class to list similarities and differences between the two. Print off the two photographs and the 'OS map of Oban' and 'OS map of Arinagour' (provided on the CD), and produce a display on which the children's list can be placed.

Arinagour pier and ferry

This is the New Pier. It was built during the 1970s. The New Pier is the biggest of the three piers, as there is also a Middle Pier and a small Old Pier right in the heart of the village of Arinagour. The Middle Pier is where smaller boats, including the fishing boats, tie up and dock. The New Pier is located furthest away from the village and is where the large ferry docks.

Both local residents and tourists use the ferry service, as it is the only way to reach the mainland from the island. Some islanders never leave the island, but those who do travel by ferry to go on holiday, to visit people, to go to the dentist and to pick up supplies from the mainland. On some days, there is a period of two hours between the arrival and departure of the ferry so people can visit Coll for a day trip.

The ferry terminal itself (shown on the right of the photograph) is a one-story building with a small office for Calmac staff, a waiting room and toilets. There are no catering facilities for travellers, but there is a burger van nearby (which is only open during the summer).

Discussing the photograph
▶ Ask the children to look at the photograph and identify the New Pier, the ferry, the ferry terminal, the sea and land.
▶ Explain that the ferry terminal is very small. While some of the ferries can hold many passengers, only about 7000 visit the island over the course of each year (of which only about 4000 are tourists).
▶ Ask the children if any of them have ever travelled by ferry to their holiday destination. Where did they travel from and to? How long did it take? How does the ferry terminal compare with the one at Coll?

Activities

▶ Give the children copies of 'Journey times' on photocopiable page 44.

▶ Explain to the children that when Barnaby Bear goes to Brittany, he travels by ferry to France. Read the book *Barnaby Bear Goes to Brittany* with the children.

▶ Help the children to use the Internet to find out how long it takes Barnaby Bear to cross the English Channel by ferry.

▶ Show the children the photograph of the 'Ferry office worker' (provided on the CD) and explain that the lady works in the terminal building.

Video: ferry at Arinagour

This video shows a morning arrival and departure, to and from Coll (Arinagour). This was filmed at the end of the summer season. A mix of locals and tourists can be seen departing from Coll. The locals will be visiting the mainland for holiday, business or personal reasons and the holidaymakers are returning home.

Typically when the ferry arrives, passengers just drive, walk or cycle off the boat, having first handed over their boarding card to a Caledonian MacBrayne official at the ferry terminal. It is then only about half a mile into the village.

The island may seem quite bleak and desolate on arrival, especially as there is little in the way of sign posting or tourist directions at the terminal. However, once visitors start exploring, there is much to be seen and appreciated. Note that the refuse truck comes to the island on a regular basis to take the rubbish and other waste away to a landfill site on the mainland.

Discussing the video

▶ Play the video to the children and ask them the following questions while it plays.

▶ Where has this been filmed?

▶ Who might be arriving on the island today and why?

▶ What do the children think their first impressions of the island might be?

▶ Who might be leaving the island today and why?

▶ What sounds can be heard on the video?

▶ What is the weather like on the video?

▶ How many different types of transport can the children spot?

▶ Can they remember where the boat has travelled from (Oban)?

▶ Where is it destined for next (Oban)?

▶ Have they ever been on a boat or ferry? Did they drive on with their family (like the car does at the end of this video), or did they walk on? What was it like?

Activities

▶ Show the video again and give small groups a theme, such as pier, ferry, people or weather. Ask the groups to remember/record anything they see on the film which relates to their theme and then to share their findings as a class.

Aeroplane to Tiree

Another route to Coll is from Glasgow by air on a small aeroplane (shown in the photograph). The flight is from Glasgow to Tiree and then a ferry departs from Tiree to Coll. Tiree is not much bigger than Coll in terms of land mass, but it is more populous (over 700 compared with 160 on Coll). Tiree also attracts tourists for its windsurfing and is a better known resort than Coll.

Discussing the picture

▶ Remind the children of the route from the mainland to Coll, which involves flying from Glasgow to Tiree. Explain that the photograph shows the type of aeroplane used.

▶ Ask the children how they would feel about travelling on such a small aeroplane.

▶ Have any of the children been on a plane before? What was it like? How was it the same or different from this plane?

Activities

▶ Using a simple atlas, map or the children's own knowledge, identify the airport closest to their locality. Has anyone flown from this airport?

▶ Help the children to use the Internet to work out whether they would be able to fly to Glasgow

from their local airport and how long it would take. Using the 'British Isles map' (provided on the CD) and prior learning, ask the children to estimate the total length of the journey from their local airport to Coll, via Glasgow and Tiree.

PEOPLE ON COLL

The following resources are best used together to allow the children to compare and contrast the different jobs people do on Coll. These images can also be matched up to the pictures of buildings on Coll to develop an understanding of where jobs are done.

Tamara Hedderwick

This photograph shows Tamara Hedderwick at the pottery she owns and runs on the Isle of Coll. She is the daughter of Mairi Hedderwick, the author of the Katie Morag stories, and has lived on the island for most of her life. Her pottery is situated within a large building beside the New Pier, where the boats come in. Pottery is sold both to local residents and to tourists, the raw material being local clay and clay imported from mainland suppliers. Tamara also holds pottery classes.

Tamara is passionate about facilities for islanders being improved, especially for the children. This includes improved transport, particularly in terms of access to the mainland for secondary school pupils and their parents. Tamara would also like to see more affordable housing, so that local people have opportunites to buy property on the island. As an artist she is also interested in creative activities to help enrich the lives of local people and those visiting the island.

Discussing the photograph
▶ Discuss with the children who is in the photograph.
▶ Ask the children what they think Tamara is doing. Explain that this is her job and that she owns the pottery on the Isle of Coll.
▶ Explain how well situated the pottery is to receive raw materials (clay) from the mainland.
▶ Ask the children to look at the photograph and to describe what they think she makes at the pottery. Explain that both local people and tourists buy her pottery and paintings.

Activities
▶ Use the 'Mairi Hedderwick' photocopiable on page 46 and explain who Tamara is.
▶ As a class, compile a list of questions for Tamara about the Isle of Coll. The children could use the 'Isle of Struay word cards' on photocopiable page 42 to help them frame their questions.
▶ Let the children use relevant websites (such as www.isleofcoll.org) and this CD to research answers to their questions. They could go on to evaluate which sources were most useful and relevant in helping them in their enquiries.

Tourists on Coll

This photograph was taken at Hogh Bay, near the castles. Around 7000 passengers arrive at Coll each year, but many are locals or are connected with the Project Trust (the Coll-based gap-year charity). A more accurate estimate of tourists would probably be closer to about 4000 a year.

Tourists tend to stay in their own holiday homes, bed and breakfast accommodation, guest houses, the hotel, flats in the village, or they camp in tents or caravans.

There is a good range of tourist attractions on the island: the beaches, sand dunes and coastal walks; wildlife, including birds, whales, sharks, dolphins and otters; fishing trips for trout in the lochs. Tourists tend to visit between April and October when the weather is better.

Tourism is a very important activity on the island and is connected with many of the other businesses. For example, Tamara's pottery retails to both local residents and to tourists. Even those who do not make a living directly from tourism are dependent on the revenue to some extent, as it helps to maintain the island's facilities and amenities.

Discussing the photograph
▶ Ask the children what they notice in the foreground of the photograph (wild flowers and people). Explain that the people are tourists, who have come to visit the island.
▶ Ask the children what they can see in the background (low-lying hills, waves, a few buildings). Explain that these features are what make Coll an attractive place to visit on holiday – a tranquil, remote island characterised by beautiful coastlines.

▶ Ask the children to comment on what the tourists are wearing and what this tells them about the weather when the photograph was taken.

Activities
▶ Using the 'OS map of Coll' (provided on the CD), ask the children to locate Hogh Bay (it's on the west of the island).
▶ Make a list of activities the children would like to do if they were to visit Coll on holiday. What do they think other members of their family would like to do?
▶ Show this picture in conjunction with 'Coll inland' (provided on the CD) to reinforce what the landscape is like on Coll.

Postman

Frank the postman picks up and delivers the post for the whole island. His delivery route comprises a road down to the west and a road up to the east. However, because there is a two-mile stretch of sand (see 'OS map of Coll', provided on the CD), Frank has to drive back around the loop to get up to the east. There are nine postboxes on the island and it takes Frank about four hours to complete his round. He is also part of the coastguard. Frank has lived on the island for about 20 years.

Discussing the photograph
▶ Explain who is in the picture to the children and tell them what he does.
▶ What do they think Frank delivers the post in? (Point out the red van in the background.)

Activities
▶ Using the 'Simple map of Coll' and the 'OS map of Coll' (provided on the CD), ask the children what they think Frank's route would be. Give each child a copy of one of the maps and ask them to mark where they think the nine postboxes should be.
▶ Invite a local postman/woman to talk to the children about their job. The children could produce a list of questions in advance, asking about the route they take and how they travel.
▶ As a class, investigate the journey of a letter to Coll. Ask the visiting postman about this and perhaps also contact the nearest sorting office for more information. The post office also deals with queries online.
▶ Give the children a copy of 'Postman' on photocopiable page 47.

Teacher

This is the pre-five teacher at Arinagour primary school, working with a small group of children. She also lives on the Isle of Coll.

Discussing the photograph
▶ Explain who is in the picture to the children and tell them what she does.
▶ Ask the children how similar this scene is to one in their own school.

Activities
▶ Ask the children to produce a simple questionnaire for teachers in their own school, to find out where they live, how they travel to school, how long it takes.
▶ The children could produce a pictogram to show some of the results.
▶ Start a 'job centre' display for Coll and the children's locality. They could add photographs and people profiles. For example, a teacher at their own school and the teacher from Arinagour primary school.

Farmer

This is a farmer on Coll. He raises livestock and grows crops. He has lived on the island for about 15 years.

Discussing the photograph
▶ Show the children the photograph and ask if they can guess what the man's job is. What clues are there to indicate that he is a farmer?

▶ Focus on his clothes. Ask the children why they think he needs to wear those particular clothes. Ask the children what they think he is carrying.

Activities
▶ Using the 'Simple map of Coll' (provided on the CD), ask the children where they think the farmer may be working (anywhere near the sheep symbols).
▶ Plan a visit to a local farm so that the children can compare this with the farm on Coll. Ask the children questions, such as What type of farm is it? How many people work here?
▶ The children could annotate a base plan of the farm they visit to show what activities occur where and by whom.

Caravan owner

This lady runs a caravan park for tourists. She is also an artist and specialises in glass painting. She has lived on the island for about ten years.

Discussing the photograph
▶ Explain who is in the photograph to the children and tell them what she does.
▶ Ask the children if they can think of other types of accommodation there might be on Coll (holiday homes, B&Bs, guest houses, a hotel, flats in the village, camping).

Activities
▶ Ask the children about accommodation they have stayed in on holiday – has anyone ever stayed in a caravan?
▶ Give the children a copy of 'Caravan owner' on photocopiable page 48.

Ferry office worker

This ferry office worker handles transactions when ferries are arriving or departing. She also helps with enquiries. She has lived on the island for about two years.

Discussing the photograph
▶ Explain to the children who is in the picture and tell them what she does.

Activities
▶ See activities for 'Arinagour pier and ferry', above.

BUILDINGS ON COLL
It is recommended that the resources which follow are used together to allow the children to compare and contrast the different buildings on Coll and their uses.

Hotel

This is the only hotel on Coll and is situated in the village of Arinagour, at the head of Loch Eatharna. There are six rooms. The hotel has been established for over 100 years. It is a family run hotel, usually at its busiest from mid-July to mid-August, and at Christmas and New Year.

Discussing the photograph
▶ Tell the children that this is the only hotel on Coll and it is in the village of Arinagour.
▶ Explain that there are various buildings on the island and this is one of the places where people visiting the island will come to stay.
▶ Tell the children that it has six rooms and is run by a family. When do the children think the hotel will be most busy?
▶ Have any of the children stayed in a hotel when they have been on holiday? What was it like in comparison to the Isle of Coll Hotel? Was it bigger or smaller?

Activities
▶ Ask the children to imagine what the hotel is like inside. Let them use the website for the hotel (www.collhotel.com) to find out more.

▶ Supervised, let the children look at tourist information from the Internet (www.isleofcoll.org or www.visitscotland.com) or, as a class, write to the tourist information office in Scotland for information about Coll.

▶ Provide the children with options on accommodation in Coll – where would they stay?

▶ Ask the children to plan a basic itinerary for a trip to Coll. They should focus on the route, mode of transport, where to stay and what to do. Give them appropriate resources from the Resource Gallery on the CD to help them.

▶ On the basis of their planned itinerary, the children could write a list of things to pack for their trip. This should include items relevant to weather and the activities they would like to do.

House

This house is situated down West End Road (on the west side of Coll). Typically, a mix of traditional stone cottages and farmhouses can be found on Coll. Within the village of Arinagour there are contrasts in terms of houses of different ages; modern semi-detached houses,; traditional rows of stone terraced houses; 'new builds' in stone cladding. There are also a few flats in the village of Arinagour and some wooden cabins. Overall, there are approximately 90 houses on the island.

Discussing the photograph

▶ Ask the children what the photograph shows and tell them where this house is.

▶ Talk about what the house is made of and whether the children think it is old or modern.

▶ Ask the children what number they live at on their street. Discuss how this house sits alone to develop ideas about how populous Coll is in comparison to the school locality.

Activities

▶ Show the children which part of the island the house is located on the 'OS map of Coll' (provided on the CD).

▶ Compare this house to the homes in the 'Barnaby Bear's local area: Chester' Resource Gallery so that the children can create a display of different homes.

▶ Photograph a range of houses in the local area when on a fieldwork walk with the children. Use them to produce a classroom 'parallel places' display to match each photograph from Coll.

Local shop

This shop is the only shop on Coll and is located in the village of Arinagour. The range of products sold here include general provisions (such as tinned goods), fruit, vegetables, dairy produce, bread, cakes, meat, fresh fish, frozen foods, cereals and essential general items such as soap and shampoo. The shop is open from about 9.30am until 1pm on some days and until 5.30pm on other days. It closes on Sundays. It is a family shop run by a couple and there are three part-time staff. Local produce includes vegetables, some fruit and eggs. Otherwise the shop manager 'drives' (via the ferry) over to the mainland about twice a week to buy stock.

Discussing the photograph

▶ Tell the children that this photograph shows the only shop on the Isle of Coll and that it is in Arinagour.

▶ Can the children tell you if the shop is open or closed in the photograph? Explain that it is open every day apart from Sundays, but not all night and day like some shops on the mainland.

▶ Ask the children to imagine that they live on the island. What do they think they would need to buy in the shop?

▶ Talk about the various products that they could buy from this shop. Explain that the shop sells a lot of local produce, such as vegetables, some fruit and eggs, but that the manager has to go to the mainland to buy other things to sell.

▶ Note all the notices in the window. Explain that because this is the only shop on the island, it means that everyone will need to come here at some point. Therefore the shop is a good place to put up notices that might be of interest to the community.

Activities

▶ Ask the children, as a homework activity, to search for two products at home that have originated from other places and ask them to bring these into school.

▶ Using a digital camera, ask the children to photograph the various items and to write their place of origin next to the photograph.

▶ Help the children to locate on a world map the various places where the food has been imported from. Emphasise the nature of interdependence between countries and the degree to which different climate and physical geography within specific locations can impact on what can be grown.

▶ Let the children compare this shop with the photograph of 'Local shops' in 'Barnaby Bear's local area: Chester' Resource Gallery. Why do the children think there are more shops in Barnaby Bear's local area?

Farm

This photograph was taken at the west end of the island, opposite Totronald, the RSPB Warden's house and visitor centre.

In terms of farming, most farms on Coll are concerned with cattle and sheep. Some locals keep chickens for meat and eggs, the latter both to sell and for personal consumption. Some cereals are grown, too, such as barley and root crops.

This is a very old, stone-built farmhouse and Anne Taylor, the farmer, lives here. At Anne Taylor's farm, meat, sheep and cattle are produced.

There is no market on Coll, nor is there an abattoir, so the stock has to be taken away on the boat to be sold, slaughtered and butchered elsewhere – this could be Tiree (which has an abattoir), Oban or elsewhere on the mainland.

Discussing the photograph

▶ Explain to the children that this is a photograph of a farm. Ask them if there are any clues that tells them it is a farm.

Activities

▶ Using the 'Simple map of Coll' and/or the 'OS map of Coll' (provided on the CD), show the children where the farm is located.

▶ Show the children various images of farms in England and discuss what happens in them. The Farming and Countryside Education website (www.face-online.org.uk) is a good source for further information about farms. For instance, dairy farming, livestock breeding, growing organic or non-organic fruit and vegetables all take place on farms. Begin to explain that different products can be farmed and ask the children to match caption cards to relevant pictures.

▶ If possible, arrange a field visit to a local farm so that the children can explore the above and other aspects of farms.

Primary school

This school is up the hill from Arinagour village. There are 25 children in the school, including four children in the pre-five nursery. There is one big classroom divided into groups for the P1–P7 children. There is a separate, smaller classroom for the pre-five children. The school has one head teacher and three assistant teachers.

Secondary school

The secondary school is at Oban on the mainland. It is near An Dunan. The children on Coll stay at the hostel there and come back every five or six weeks. Occasionally, a boat will not be able to call into Coll because of the weather, so a child might miss a few days of school, but because they are not making a daily commute the chances of this are relatively low. There are not enough children on the Isle of Coll to justify the building of a secondary school.

Discussing the photographs

▶ Show the children the two photographs together and explain that these are both schools: one is a primary school (like their own) and the other is a secondary school.

▶ Ask the children to talk about the similarities and differences between the two schools (the main one being that the high school is a lot bigger).

▶ How does the Arinagour primary school compare with the children's own school? Does it look bigger or smaller?

Activities
▶ Using the 'OS map of Arinagour' and 'OS map of Oban', point out where the schools are.
▶ Compare the photograph of Arinagour primary school with that of 'Barnaby Bear's school: entrance' from the 'Barnaby Bear's local area: Chester' Resource Gallery. Do the children think the two schools are similar or different?
▶ Using a map of their own locality, ask the children to find their school.

SOUNDS OF COLL

Audio: Hebridean music

This piece of music is called 'Co Ni Mire Rium?' and has been taken from the album *Grace and Pride: The Anthology 1984–2004* by Capercaillie. The track is sung in Gaelic. Although this song is not from Coll, it is typical of music from the Hebrides. The full lyrics and translation can be found at Capercaillie's website (www.capercaillie.co.uk).

Discussing the music and activities
▶ Play the music through once to the class. Ask the children to listen carefully to the extract and to note which words come to mind when listening to it.
▶ In small groups, ask the children to listen to the track again. Using thumbnails of images from the Resource Gallery, ask them to select which photographs seem to best 'match' the music. Each group should choose three and explain their reasons.

Audio: waves

This track has been recorded on a beach in Coll. You can hear the sea lapping. Tourists enjoy walking and cycling along the beaches and bays here.

Audio: seagulls

This track has also been recorded on a beach in Coll. The seagulls can be heard here. There is a nature reserve on the island (see the 'OS map of Coll', provided on the CD).

Audio: sheep

This track has been recorded on a farm in Coll. Sheep and cattle farming are the most common types of farming on the island.

Discussing the sounds and activities
▶ Play the three sounds to the children and ask them to draw a picture to show where they think these sounds were recorded.
▶ Record some sounds in the local area and repeat the first activity with the children.
▶ In small groups, ask the children to record sounds around the school, photographing where these sounds are recorded. Groups could then exchange sounds and photographs and try to match them up. Alternatively, groups could exchange their sounds and predict where they think the sounds were recorded before matching them up with the photographs.
▶ Ask the children to rank the three sounds on the CD in order of preference and to explain reasons for their choices.

NOTES ON THE PHOTOCOPIABLE PAGES

Word cards   PAGE 42

These cards show key words for describing the features of an island that children will encounter when working on the unit. Encourage the children to use the word cards in displays using the maps and pictures in the Resource Gallery, and to help them when talking and writing about the pictures. The children can build their own word bank by thinking of other words for features on an island.

Activities
▶ Cut out the cards and laminate them. Use the word cards as often as possible when talking about the Isle of Coll and the Isle of Struay.
▶ Let the children match the word cards to the pictures in the Resource Gallery.

Map symbols   PAGE 43

Emphasise the importance of map symbols to the children. Tell them that they are necessary because it would be difficult to show features exactly as they are on a map. This drawing frame can be used with both the 'Simple map of Coll' and the 'OS map of Coll' (provided on the CD).

Activities
▶ Give the children a copy of either of the maps of Coll and read out the features on the photocopiable sheet to them. Ask them to find the features and draw them in the boxes. Remind them to use the right colours and talk about why particular colours are used.
▶ Devise a similar drawing frame for other maps.

Journey times   PAGE 44

It takes approximately two hours and forty-five minutes for the ferry to travel from Oban to Coll, although the times do vary in the spring/summer and autumn/winter seasons. Use this sheet as a starting point to investigate other journey times and to develop the children's ability to tell the time using a clock face.

Activities
▶ Ask the children to tell the times on the two clocks. Point to the arrows to show how the positions indicate the time. Talk about the different ways of saying what the time is. For example, 06.45 can also be a 'quarter to seven'.
▶ Work out with the children how long the journey takes. Use a toy clock if one is available.
▶ Ask the children to time how long it takes them to make particular journeys. For example, from home to school. Ask them to record times in numbers and draw the times on a clock face.

Living on Coll   PAGE 45

Use this writing frame to investigate the physical and human features of Coll through the use of enquiry questions. Encourage the children to use appropriate geographical vocabulary, such as hilly, flat, rocky, and so on. These skills can be applied to other locality studies.

Activities
▶ Ask the children to work in small groups or individually to complete this writing frame. Use pictures from the Resource Gallery to support the children if appropriate. Compare and contrast what each child or group has written.
▶ Split the children into four or eight groups and ask the groups to focus on one of the aspects of life on Coll instead of all four.

Mairi Hedderwick, Postman, Caravan Owner   PAGES 46-48

These texts are profiles of Mairi Hedderwick (author of the Katie Morag books) and two residents on the Isle of Coll: Frank the Postman and Karlijn (pronounced 'Kar-lin'), a caravan owner.

Activities
▶ The profiles talk about what the people do and how they are connected to Coll. Use these texts for extended discussion when using the resources about the people on Coll in the Resource Gallery.
▶ Read the profiles with the children. Talk about what these three people do.
▶ Help the children to make a similar profile of someone they know. They could use a photograph, draw a picture or use a digital camera to illustrate their text. This work could be used in a display of people in the local area.

Isle of Struay word cards

island
bay
lighthouse
village
port
shop
post office
High Farm

Map symbols

- Can you find these symbols and features on the map?
- Draw them in the boxes and colour them in.

Lighthouse	
Road	
Bird sanctuary	
Beach	
Lake	
Stream	

Journey times

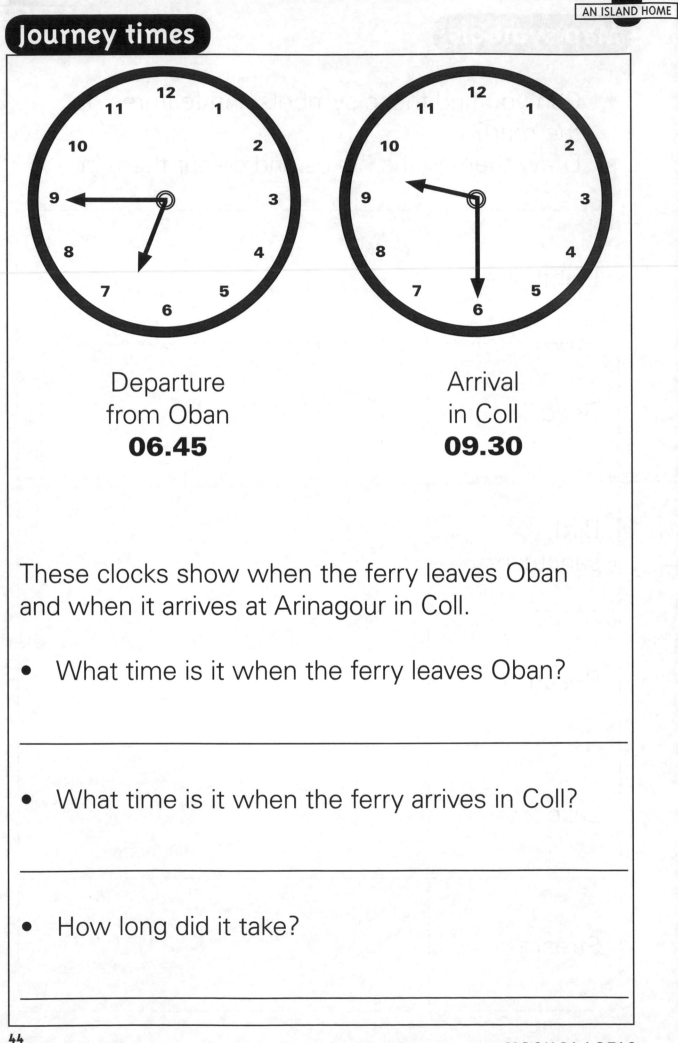

Departure
from Oban
06.45

Arrival
in Coll
09.30

These clocks show when the ferry leaves Oban and when it arrives at Arinagour in Coll.

- What time is it when the ferry leaves Oban?

_____

- What time is it when the ferry arrives in Coll?

_____

- How long did it take?

_____

Living on Coll

Landscape

What is the landscape like here? Is it flat or hilly?

Buildings

Are there many buildings on Coll? What sort of buildings?

Land use

What is the land used for here?

Jobs people do

What jobs do people do here? Why?

SCHOLASTIC
PHOTOCOPIABLE

READY RESOURCES ▶▶ GEOGRAPHY

Mairi Hedderwick

- Mairi Hedderwick was born in Gourock, Scotland. She learned to draw and paint at the Edinburgh College of Art, and was a teacher before she became a writer.

- Her first Katie Morag book was published in 1984. It was called *Katie Morag Delivers the Mail*. There are 16 more stories in the series including *Katie Morag and the Two Grandmothers* and *Katie Morag and the New Pier*. Katie Morag lives on the Isle of Struay, which is not a real place but is based on Mairi's life on the Isle of Coll as a mother and now a grandmother. When Mairi visits schools she sometimes has Katie Morag's teddy in her travel bag – if Katie Morag will let her.

Postman

- This is Frank the Postman. He picks up and delivers the mail for the whole of the Isle of Coll. There are three post boxes on the island and it takes Frank about four hours to complete his mail round. Frank picks mail up from the ferry, then drives all round the island delivering to all of the houses. (He doesn't visit every house, as some have a mailbox where their track meets the road).

- As well as being the postman, Frank is also part of the coastguard. This means that he carries a pager and is on standby for being called out to help if there is an accident at sea.

- Frank has lived on the island for about 20 years, having moved from Fife with his wife and children.

Photo © Pete MacKay www.isleofcoll.org

Caravan owner

- This is Karlijn, who owns a caravan which is available as holiday accommodation for tourists. Some of her guests are people who have been coming to Coll for years, others are first-timers who have perhaps heard about Coll from friends or the Isle of Coll website. Out of the tourist season, like many people on Coll with spare accommodation, Karlijn takes in volunteers for Project Trust, a gap-year charity based on Coll.

- Karlijn is also an artist and freelance translator. She specialises in glass painting, usually Celtic designs and images from nature.

- Karlijn is originally from Holland, but has lived on Coll for nine years and is raising her family here.

GOING TO THE SEASIDE

Photodisc via SODA

Content and skills
This chapter supports the activities in unit 4, 'Going to the seaside', of the QCA Scheme of Work for geography at Key Stage 1. This unit is set mainly in a geographical context which uses a historical perspective to help children understand how seaside places have evolved over time. This chapter supports the QCA unit by providing some of the necessary resources for investigation of human and physical features in seaside locations. The content augments and extends the QCA unit by looking at a range of different coastal locations and by focusing on a specific seaside place – the resort of Tenby in South Wales. Specific resources deal with seaside sports, physical features, transport and fishing. Use of the content will aid the development of children's visual literacy skills and, specifically, their ability to gather information from maps.

Resources on the CD-ROM
The resources include images of a seaside resort – Tenby – now and in the past. There are also images showing different types of seaside places – beaches of shingle and sand, a ferry port and a fishing port. One image highlights the issue of litter on the coast. Different types of maps and an aerial photograph will contribute to the development of children's geographical understanding and skills.

Photocopiable pages
The photocopiable resources within the book will enable the children to organise and communicate their findings about the seaside. The sheets are also designed to develop children's data handling and thinking skills. In addition, the sheets are provided in PDF format on the CD-ROM and include:
► word cards
► an odd-one-out activity to develop thinking skills
► an activity to compare sand and shingle beaches
► a chart to help in categorising seaside sports and activities
► diagrams showing different types of fishing boats and nets
► a litter survey.

Geographical skills
Skills developed by activities using the resources in this chapter include map reading and interpretation, identification of key features within visual images, data handling and the development of geographical vocabulary.

NOTES ON THE CD-ROM RESOURCES

British Isles' coastline

This map shows the British Isles with countries labelled. It clearly shows that mainland Britain and Ireland are islands with extensive coastlines. It also shows the many smaller islands that make up the British Isles, from the Scilly Isles in the south to Shetland in the north.

Discussing the map
▶ Ask the children to identify the countries that make up the British Isles.
▶ Ask the children to identify the country that they live in.
▶ Ask selected children to give their addresses. Write one on the board and break the address down into its constituent parts. Explain that the further down the address an item is, the larger the area it describes. For example, 'Lancashire' is a larger area than 'Blackpool', which is a larger area than 'Church Road'. Explain that the name of the country will always be at the foot of an address, because it is the name of a very large area taking in many counties and towns.

Activities
▶ Print out copies of the map and ask the children to mark the school's locality.
▶ Get the children to use a wall map, road atlas maps or the 'Get-a-map' service on the Ordnance Survey website (www.ordnancesurvey.co.uk) to identify some seaside places that they know in the British Isles. Mark some of these locations on a printed copy of the map.
▶ Print out the map and write some of the words on the 'Seaside word cards', on photocopiable pages 59 and 60, around the coast. Ask the children to find pictures of seaside places in the British Isles from holiday brochures and to collage the pictures around the map.

Shingle beach

Beaches made of shingle (accumulations of small, smooth, rounded pebbles) are usually narrower and steeper than sandy beaches. This beach, at Birling Gap in Sussex on the south coast of England, is backed by high, white cliffs made of chalk (the 'Seven Sisters') and has a steep gradient. There is a pebble bank at the rear of the beach to protect the cliffs from erosion and, except at times of very high tide and stormy weather, is a stable feature. Further down the beach, however, the pebbles are in constant motion – moved back and forth by the tide and along the beach by wave action. Although there are people sunbathing in the photograph, shingle beaches are notoriously uncomfortable to lie and to walk on. People can also damage shingle beaches. Walking on the pebbles cause them to slip and slide, leaving gaps in the pebble bank which the waves can penetrate.

Discussing the photograph
▶ Ask the children to list the features they can see in the photograph, such as cliff and beach.
▶ Discuss the appearance of the beach. Ask the children how this beach is similar or different to other beaches they have seen.
▶ What do the children think the beach is made of?
▶ Ask them what people in the photograph appear to be doing. Does the beach appear to be good for sunbathing and other beach activities? Could they build a sandcastle there?

Activities
▶ Let the children feel a collection of small pebbles, like those found on a shingle beach. If pebbles from a beach are not available, then ones from a stream or decorative pebbles from a garden centre will do. Encourage the children to come up with words to describe the texture and sounds made when the pebbles come into contact with others.
▶ Compare the photograph to those of 'Penally Beach' and 'North Beach' (provided on the CD). Ask the children to list the similarities and differences. Which beach would they prefer to visit? Why?

Windsurfers

Windsurfing is a popular sport, especially on exposed stretches of coast, where windsurfers can use the wind to send their boards skimming or 'planing' across the surface of the water. It began in the late 1960s, when two Californians, a sailor and a surfer, patented the first 'windsurfer' – a surfboard with a sail (called a rig) attached via a universal joint. The design was unique because it allowed the tilting of the rig backwards and forwards to steer without the use of a rudder. After a slow start, sailboarding (as it was then called) became a highly popular activity in North America and in Europe. In 1984, it became an Olympic sport.

Windsurfers can use their boards even in light winds and, contrary to popular belief, it is not a hugely expensive or particularly dangerous sport. In the UK, favourite windsurfing beaches face south-west (to catch prevailing winds) and have waves running parallel to the shore for at least part of their length. Places to see windsurfing include Rhosneigr on Anglesey, Gwithian Beach in Cornwall and Prestwick in Scotland.

Other sports which children may see at seaside locations include yachting, dinghy sailing, sand-yachting, waterskiing and surfing. Most make use of the combination of sand, sea and wind at the coast. Some are 'adrenalin sports' with an element of danger caused by speed over water or sand.

Discussing the photograph

▶ Ask the children what they can see in the photograph. What are the objects on the beach and how are they used? Point out the windsurfers at sea in the background.

▶ If the children do not know the terms, introduce the words windsurfer and windsurfing. Point out the two elements of the activity: 'wind' and 'surfing'.

▶ Ask the children why they think windsurfers like this place. (Winds, sandy beach, shallow sea.)

▶ Ask the children about any other sporting activities they may have seen at seaside locations. Point out that many of these activities make use of the wind. Why do they think the seaside is often a windy place?

Activities

▶ Ask the children for a list of words to describe the scene in the photograph. Get them to focus on the colours and details in the foreground, middle and background. Ask the children to give the photograph a title.

▶ As a class, list words to describe what it might feel like to windsurf. Prompt the children to think about the sounds they might hear, and the feel of the board and the wind.

▶ Get the children to list and draw pictures of other seaside sports.

Ferry port

This photograph shows the port of Dover in Kent, with ferries being loaded and unloaded. A ferry is a ship that transports people and/or vehicles across a body of water and operates on a regular schedule. Ferry services operate from ports all around the UK, linking Britain to Ireland, France, Spain, Belgium, the Netherlands and Scandinavia. The English Channel has many ferry services, with Dover being the busiest port, largely because it offers the shortest routes to France.

Dover ferries are designed for a fast turnaround at either end of their relatively short journey across the English Channel. They have huge watertight doors which open as soon as the ship arrives in port. Cars and lorries roll on and roll off the ferries (hence the term 'Ro-Ro' ferries) in a matter of minutes.

Although the building of the Channel Tunnel has reduced some of the traffic, ferries remain a highly popular way of crossing the Channel, especially for shoppers who want to carry large quantities of goods in their cars.

A recent innovation on some ferry routes has been the introduction of fast ferries: single- or double-hulled, turbine-powered craft which skim across the water at high speed. They have reduced journey times dramatically on some routes. For example, the fast ferry from Stranraer in Scotland to Belfast in Northern Ireland takes 1 hour and 45 minutes, while the conventional ferry takes over three hours.

Discussing the photograph

▶ Ask the children what they can see in the photograph. Ask them to identify physical as well as human features. Encourage them to describe the cliffs in the background.

▶ Point out the features on the nearest ship – the funnels, the rows of windows indicating several decks, the lifeboats and the bridge. Explain that the ships in the photograph are called ferries, and that these ferries carry people and vehicles across the English Channel to France.

▶ What do the children think the weather is like in the photograph? Point out clues, such as the clouds and the state of the sea.
▶ Ask the children if the nearest ferry has just arrived or is about to leave.

Activities
▶ Identify the English Channel on a map of the UK or Europe. Point out the location of Dover and ask the children why they think it is a popular ferry port.
▶ Print out copies of the photograph and ask the children to work in groups to label it. Features they can label include the cliffs, the quays and the different parts of the ferry.
▶ The Port of Dover has a very comprehensive website (www.doverport.co.uk). Although not aimed at children, the virtual tour feature gives a good sense of what it is like to board and travel by ferry. It also gives sea conditions in the Channel.
▶ Some UK wall maps (and all road atlases) show the ferry routes in and out of ports around the coast. Get the children to record all the ferry routes they can find. Ask them to find the longest and the shortest routes. The websites www.poferries.com and www.stenaline.co.uk provide lots of information on routes.

FISHING

Fishing boat

This image and the following one show two very different kinds of fishing boats. This photograph shows a scene at Chesil Beach in Dorset with a traditional seine net fishing boat, called a lerret, in the background. Seine netting is a type of inshore fishing used mainly to catch mackerel. A seine net hangs vertically in the water with stones attached at the bottom and floating corks at the top – fish swim into the net and are trapped by their gills. A lerret, with a pointed bow at each end, is rowed away from the beach with the net being thrown or 'shot' from the rear. A rope, attached to the net, remains on land with a beach crew. The lerret is rowed in a wide, semi-circular course back to the beach and the boat end of the net is brought ashore by the boat crew. The hard work of pulling in the seine then begins – boat and beach crews pull together and slowly the net is brought ashore. If the skipper is lucky, he will find that he has trapped a shoal of mackerel in the net. On some days, however, the net might only contain a few fish and a lot of seaweed!

The photograph shows that this lerret has made a good catch. The seine has been brought ashore and the fisherman in the foreground is taking the fish from the net. Traditionally the catch would have been placed in large wicker baskets to be taken up the beach. The photograph shows the mackerel being placed in boxes, however, ready to be covered in ice to keep them fresh. Seine netting is still practiced in the summer at Chesil Beach, with stones from the beach continuing to be used as weights for the nets.

Discussing the photograph
▶ Ask them what type of beach this appears to be. Is it sand or shingle?
▶ Ask them to describe the boat. Focus on its size and how many people it might carry. Explain that it is called a lerret. What do they think the boat is used for?
▶ Ask the children what the person in the foreground is doing. Explain that he is removing fish from a net and putting them in boxes ready to take to a market or to local shops.
▶ Ask the children whether they think the fish have been caught near the shore or far out to sea. The size of the boat is a clue.

Activities
See the activities for 'Trawler', below.

Trawler

This photograph shows in-shore trawlers moored up at the fish quay at Bridlington on the Yorkshire coast. Although much larger than the lerrets of Chesil Beach, they are relatively small when compared to the deep-sea trawlers that catch fish off Iceland. The nets they use are very different to seines. Trawlers use huge, bag-shaped nets that are dragged along the sea bottom. The open end of the net is kept open by floats and weights in a similar way to the seine, but

there the similarity ends. Trawlers stay at sea for several days at a time and may travel hundreds of miles in search of deep-sea fish, such as cod. The boats in the photograph have recently had their catches unloaded – note the stacked boxes and the lorry waiting on the quay. They are characteristic of this type of craft – brightly painted with high bows and wheelhouses in the middle.

Discussing the photograph

▶ Ask the children to compare these boats to the photograph of the 'Fishing boat'. What are the similarities and differences?

▶ Ask the children to describe the place where these boats are moored. Is it a beach? Explain that this is a fishing port and that the boats are tied up to a quay in a harbour.

▶ Ask the children to describe the boats. Draw their attention to the high bows, the wheelhouses and the masts with radio aerials. Why do they think the trawlers are painted in bright colours?

▶ Do the children think that these boats stay close to the shore, like the lerret, or go further out to sea?

Activities

▶ As a class, make a chart comparing the two different types of fishing boat in the photographs. Compare their size, the materials they are made from, their shape, the distance they travel from the coast and how fish are brought to shore.

▶ Ask the children to list any different kinds of fish they know of and different ways in which fish is served as food (fish fingers, fish and chips, fisherman's pie). There are activities on the Seafish Authority's education website (www.seafish-education.org.uk) which may help to prompt the children's thinking.

▶ Give the children a copy of the 'Fishing boats' photocopiable on page 64 to complete.

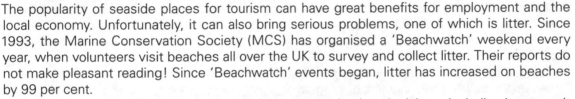

Seaside litter

The popularity of seaside places for tourism can have great benefits for employment and the local economy. Unfortunately, it can also bring serious problems, one of which is litter. Since 1993, the Marine Conservation Society (MCS) has organised a 'Beachwatch' weekend every year, when volunteers visit beaches all over the UK to survey and collect litter. Their reports do not make pleasant reading! Since 'Beachwatch' events began, litter has increased on beaches by 99 per cent.

In 2003, over one third of litter recorded was sourced to beach visitors, including items such as crisp packets, sweet wrappers, plastic drinks bottles and cigarette stubs. Fishing litter, such as fishing nets and line, rope and buoys, was the second most common litter source. Although sewage-related debris was another source (the result of the continuing practice of dumping sewage in the sea from outflows), litter from ships was not a serious problem – in 2003, items such as oil drums, crates and strapping bands accounted for only 2 per cent of total litter.

Litter left at the seaside is not just unsightly, it can be dangerous. Broken glass on a beach can lead to serious injury. Birds and marine mammals can become entangled in plastic and discarded nets. So what can be done about the problem? Encouraging people to take their litter home is a first step and the MCS has a 'Seaside Code' which does just that. During the summer season, most bathing beaches are cleaned on a daily basis, but litter can become an issue out of season. The MCS runs an 'Adopt a Beach' scheme, which organises voluntary beach cleaning events throughout the year.

Discussing the photograph

▶ Ask the children if this appears to be a popular seaside place. Ask them what they can see in the foreground of the photograph. What is the link between the litter and the people?

▶ Ask the children why leaving litter like this on a beach is not a good idea. Prompt them by pointing out that people are walking with bare feet.

▶ Ask what might happen to the litter when the people have gone. (The tide might wash the litter away, thus polluting the sea, or birds might attempt to eat the litter and be harmed.)

▶ Stress that they should not touch or move litter like this on a beach. Emphasise that they can help by not dropping litter themselves, but should not touch other people's rubbish.

Activities

▶ As a class, send off for the 'Seaside Code'. This is available free (with a stamped addressed

envelope) from Marine Conservation Society, Unit 3, Wolf Business Park, Alton Road, Ross-on-Wye, Herefordshire HR9 5NB (http://www.goodbeachguide.co.uk/Info/seasidecode.htm).
▶ Get the children to design a poster encouraging people not to drop litter at the seaside.
▶ Use the 'Litter on the beach' photocopiable on page 65 to do a litter survey. As a class, make a chart or pictogram of results and ask the children to identify the main source of litter on the beach.

Family at the seaside

This photograph shows people's enthusiasm for seaside activities, regardless of the weather. The grey sky and the family's clothes indicate that this is not a warm, sunny day. The weather is not stopping them, however, from enjoying building a sandcastle on a beach of fine sand.

Beaches are depositional features. They are made up of material that has been eroded by wave action and transported along the coast by the process of longshore drift. Where softer rocks on the coast have been worn into a bay, the material accumulates to form a beach.

Longshore drift is caused by waves striking the coast at an angle. Material is pushed up a beach obliquely, but due to gravity it descends straight down meaning that progressively it moves along the coast. Wooden barriers (called groynes) are often built on beaches to slow this movement, but essentially beaches are transient features.

Local authorities at tourist resorts often spend a great deal of money maintaining their beaches and some shorelines. If left to natural processes, these would be devoid of sand were it not for the regular intervention of earth-moving machinery.

Discussing the photograph
▶ Ask the children what the people in the photograph are doing. Where are they? What kind of beach is this?
▶ Ask the children if the family appears to be enjoying their visit to the beach. What is the weather like? Is it a hot, sunny day? What clues are there that it is a cool day?
▶ Ask the children if they have ever been to a beach out of season and/or when the weather is cool? What is the seaside like at these times?

Activities
▶ Ask the children to list and/or draw pictures of activities that can be done on a sandy beach. For example, building sandcastles, digging holes, flying a kite, playing cricket or football.
▶ Carry out a survey to find out the class's favourite beach activity. Make a physical graph with cubes, a wall display or use simple data handling software to display the results. Ask the children to list questions that can be answered by the survey results. For example, What is the favourite beach activity?, What is the least popular activity? or How many more people like x than y?

OS map of Tenby

Tenby is a seaside town on Carmarthen Bay in Pembrokeshire, South Wales. Probably originating as a Viking settlement, the town grew around the now-ruined Tenby Castle as a port, and became a popular resort in the late 18th century.

Attractions in Tenby include two sandy beaches, the 13th-century town walls, the 15th-century St Mary's Church, the Tudor Merchant's House and the Pembrokeshire Coast Path which skirts the town along the seashore. Boats sail from Tenby's harbour to Caldey Island, 4.8km offshore, while St Catherine's Island is linked to the town by a causeway.

Most of these features are shown clearly on the map although, depending on the age and experience of the children in relation to map work, you may need to help them interpret the different map features.

One feature of the map that children may find puzzling is the harbour. It appears from the map to be part of the beach and, therefore, inaccessible to boats. You will need to remind or explain to children about the tide.

The tide is the regular rising and falling of the sea's surface caused by changes in gravitational forces. At any point on the coast, there are normally two high tides and two low tides each day. On average, high tides occur 12 hours and 25 minutes apart. The fact that the harbour on the map is shown as lying within the tidal range indicates that it is subject to the tides and can only be fully used by boats for two periods every day when the tide is high.

Discussing the map

▶ Begin by briefly showing the children a range of images of Tenby (from the CD). Ask the children to identify and remember the main features of this place, such as the beach, the church, boats in the harbour. Show the map to the children and ask if they can find any of the features they have seen in the photographs. They should be able to identify some more obvious features, such as beaches and the harbour.

▶ Point out the location of any features they have not been able to locate on the map, such as the symbol for a church with a spire (black circle with a cross).

▶ Ask the children if they have had any experience of the tide and explain it to them. Ask why they think the harbour in Tenby is shown as part of the beach. Point out the high and low water marks on the map (the 'MLW' (Mean Low Water) and 'MHW' (Mean High Water) labels).

Activities

▶ Put the children into groups and give each group a large sheet of paper and felt-tipped pens. Ask one member of each group to view the map of Tenby for a short time and report back to the others what they have seen. Tell them that you want each group to make simple maps of Tenby showing the main features. During the session, let each group member have a short time to view the map. The children will have to discuss, share and collaborate to create their maps. The approach should encourage the identification of key features and the formulation of simple strategies to work together. Compare the groups' maps – do all the maps show the same features?

▶ Ask the children to work individually or in pairs to create a map of either a seaside resort they have visited or an imaginary resort.

Castle Hill

This aerial photograph shows a physical feature of the coast and human features from Tenby's past: the castle and the harbour. Before its growth as a tourist resort, Tenby had several functions in the past, some of which continue today. It was an important trading port during the 14th and 15th centuries. The harbour continued to function as a port for leisure craft and as the starting point for the small ferry to Caldey Island. Close to the harbour (seen on the left of this photograph) is the boathouse and slipway for the Tenby Lifeboat. The ruins of the castle indicate that Tenby had a strategic military function in Norman times. The castle (begun in 1153), and the later town walls, guarded the coast and protected the port from incursions by native Welsh armies.

The headland is a key physical feature in that it indicates that harder, more resistant rocks meet the sea at this point. Wave action has not eroded the coast as much here, resulting in a jutting promontory, with bays made up of softer rocks on either side. Because it is beset by the sea on three sides, however, a headland will still suffer from erosion. Where there are faults and cracks at the base of cliffs, wave action will gradually undermine the cliff face and cause collapses and landslips. The cliff will very slowly and gradually retreat, leaving a flat, wave-cut platform with rocky pools exposed at low tide.

Discussing the photograph

▶ Ask the children how they think this photograph was taken.

▶ Discuss the physical and human features in the photograph. Point out the castle on the headland, the harbour and the lifeboat station.

▶ Point out the rocks on the fringes of the headland. Ask the children why this was a good place to build a castle. Can they think why the headland has not been worn away into a beach? (The rocks that make up the headland are harder than those that make up the bays on either side.)

▶ Ask the children if they think this photograph was taken at high or low tide. Point out the boats sitting on the sand and mud in the harbour.

Activities

▶ Print copies of the photograph and ask the children to work in groups to label the key features – the beach, headland, harbour, lifeboat station, coastal path.

▶ Show the children the Tenby Lifeboat website (www.tenbyrnli.co.uk). Ask them to imagine what it might be like to be on a lifeboat engaged in a rescue mission in rough seas. Ask them to list words to describe the scene and the feelings of the lifeboat crew.

TENBY AS A HOLIDAY RESORT

People on Tenby beach, Tenby harbour, North Beach

Like many seaside resorts, Tenby began to develop its facilities for visitors during the late 18th century when doctors first began to extol the virtues of sea water and sea air to their wealthy patients. Bathing, and even drinking, sea water were promoted as activities likely to cure a multitude of ills, and maintain good health and fitness. Genteel society, from places such as London and Bath, moved to Tenby in the summer months and built grand, well-proportioned Georgian houses overlooking the sea. Tenby's growth was further spurred by the Napoleonic Wars in the late 18th/early 19th centuries, which prevented wealthy people from visiting Europe. Instead of engaging in the 'Grand Tour' of European culture, they sought out scenic locations at home, with Tenby being a particular favourite because of its mild climate and picturesque setting. The opening of the railway in 1866 completed Tenby's transformation from a quietly decaying port to a thriving tourist resort. People of more modest means could now visit Tenby and stay in hotels built, following the railway opening, during the later Victorian period.

The photographs show some of Tenby's attractions for visitors now and in the past. For modern visitors, the beaches are perfect for sunbathing and beach activities. The castle and historic harbour fascinated early visitors as much as they attract visitors now.

Penally Beach

This picture shows the sandy beach that runs from Tenby's South Beach. In 2004, it won an ENCAMS Seaside Award, which means that it is well managed, clean, safe and has a high standard of bathing water. Penally is south of Tenby on the coast.

Discussing the photographs

▶ Ask the children to list the human and physical features they can see in the photographs.
▶ Ask them to identify features that might attract visitors to Tenby. Also ask them to look for evidence of places where visitors might stay.
▶ Are there any features of Tenby that can be found in the school locality? What are the similarities and differences?

Activities

▶ Ask the children to list and/or draw pictures of things they have seen or would expect to see at a seaside resort. Ask them to go through the list and indicate if the features can be seen in the photographs of Tenby. They should identify that Tenby has characteristic features, such as beaches, hotels and a harbour, but does not appear to have a pier (such as in Llandudno) or a large funfair (such as in Blackpool).
▶ Get the children to work in small groups to produce posters advertising the attractions of Tenby. The posters could be hand-drawn or collages made from printouts of images on the CD. Encourage them to feature a simple slogan, such as 'Have Fun in Tenby!'

Seaside in the past

This photograph, from the 1890s, shows the North Beach at Tenby, with many features characteristic of the late Victorian seaside. At this time Tenby had ceased to be a resort frequented only by the very wealthy. Like other resorts, it was transformed by the arrival of the railway into a centre for mass tourism – although its relatively remote location and physical features mitigated against it becoming a resort of the size or character of Blackpool or Brighton.

The features to note in the photograph include the bathing machines (huts on wheels) at the water's edge. These allowed bathers to change and enter the water with modesty and discretion. In the Victorian period, men and women wishing to enjoy the sea were segregated into separate areas, so that nobody of the opposite sex might catch sight of them in their bathing suits, which (although extremely unrevealing by today's standards) were not considered proper clothing to be seen in by the general public. Bathers entered a bathing machine away from the water's edge and changed in almost total darkness inside – complete privacy was ensured by lack of windows. The machine was pulled in and out of the water by horse power – a horse can be seen with the most distant group of machines in the photograph.

Most of the people in the photograph are 'promenading' on the sands. All appear to be dressed in their 'Sunday best' and many of the women are carrying parasols to shade them from the heat of the sun. The seaside, for the Victorians, was a place to 'take the air' and take a short dip in the sea for medicinal reasons.

Discussing the photograph

▶ Ask the children whether the photograph shows Tenby's North Beach now or in the past? How do the children know it was taken in the past?

▶ What do the children think the huts on wheels were used for? Can they see how the huts were moved up and down the beach?

▶ Ask the class what the children in the photograph are doing. Are they doing similar or different activities to ones they would do at the seaside themselves?

Activities

▶ Compare the photograph to the one of 'North Beach' now (provided on the CD). What are the similarities between the scenes? What are the differences? (There has been some additional building on the cliff top and, at the base of the cliffs, some sea defences have been added to protect the cliffs from erosion.)

▶ In groups, get the children to make a chart comparing the seaside in the past and now. They should use headings such as 'Bathing', 'Dress', 'Children's Activities'.

▶ Print out the photograph and get the children to discuss it in groups. Give each group a counter and ask individual children to put the counter on a place in the photograph. Ask them to describe to others in the group what they might see, feel and hear if they were standing on this spot on the beach in the 1890s.

NOTES ON THE PHOTOCOPIABLE PAGES

Word cards   PAGES 59-60

The cards show key words and geographical terms that children will encounter when working on this unit.

Activities

▶ Cut up the word cards and laminate them. Use them throughout the teaching of this unit to form a word bank.

▶ Let the children use the word cards to create captions for the pictures in the Resource Gallery.

Odd one out   PAGE 61

This photocopiable should be used as a focus for group discussion. It presents three distinct places in a seaside location and asks children to identify the odd one out from pictures of natural and human features/activities. It can be used as a focus for a thinking skills activity where children have to justify their choices.

Activities

▶ Ask the children to describe the items in a row of pictures and then to identify the odd one out. Ask them to give a reason why the item is not found in the given seaside location.

▶ Ask the children if there are any times when the item might be found in the location. For instance, when might a heavy lorry be seen on a beach, especially a concrete mixer?

Sandy and shingle beaches   PAGE 62

This photocopiable should be used to enable children to compare the characteristics of sandy and shingle beaches.

Activity

The children can use the chart to record their impressions of sandy and shingle beaches. Show them pictures on the CD if they need support and use any personal experiences the children have.

Water sports

PAGE 63

This sheet should help children to think about the sports and activities that they may see going on at the seaside. Some activities go on in the sea, some on the beach and some activities make use of the wind. The overlapping circles enable children to sort the sports at the bottom of the sheet into beach activities, sea activities, beach activities that use wind power and sea-based activities that use the wind.

Activities

▶ Ask the children to identify the activities shown by the pictures on the sheet.
▶ Discuss with the children where the activities take place and whether they use the wind or not. Ask the children to cut out the pictures and place them in the correct zones on the overlapping circles.

Fishing boats

PAGE 64

This sheet shows cross-section views of two different types of fishing boat and their nets – a lerret with a seine net and a trawler with a trawl net. You will need to explain to the children that all seafish (mackerel, cod, haddock, plaice) are caught in nets by fishing boats. You may also need to explain the cross-section view as it may be unfamiliar to the children. If a cross-section is an entirely new format to them, get them to copy the pictures carefully.

Activities

▶ Discuss the pictures with the children, identifying how the boats and nets are different (especially the differing sizes of the boats) and how they are similar.
▶ Get the children to identify the features that are present in both pictures (boat, floats and weights). Then ask them to identify the features that are different.

Litter on the beach

PAGE 65

This sheet is designed to enable children who do not have access to a beach location to carry out a survey of waste material on a beach. The amounts of each type of litter (from visitors, fishing and shipping) are based on data from the Beachwatch 2003 litter survey (conducted by the Marine Conservation Society).

Activities

▶ Ask the children to describe the state of the beach. Ask them to identify the items of litter and match them to the sources – visitors, the fishing boat or the ship.
▶ Get the children to tally the amounts of litter from each source. The data from this survey can then be displayed as a physical graph (using cubes) or as a simple block graph using data handling software on a computer.

© Corel

Seaside word cards

seaside
beach
coast
holiday
sand
shingle
weather
postcard

boats
ferry
harbour
fishing
windsurfing
sports
swimming
swimwear

Odd one out

- Can you spot the odd one out in these sets of pictures?
- Why is it the odd one out?

On the beach

Why? _____

In the sea

Why? _____

On the cliffs

Why? _____

Sandy and shingle beaches

Write or draw the differences between sandy and shingle beaches.

	Sandy	Shingle
	© Corel	© Corel
Wide or narrow?		
Slope		
How does it feel?		
Things to do		
Which do I like best?		

Water sports

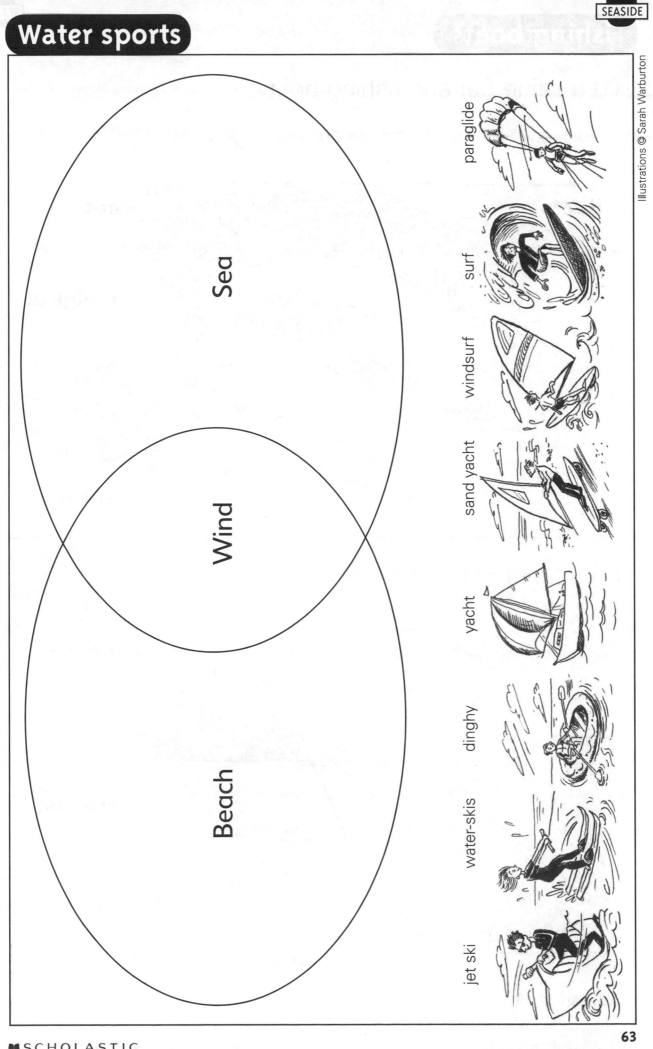

Sea

Wind

Beach

paraglide

surf

windsurf

sand yacht

yacht

dinghy

water-skis

jet ski

■ SCHOLASTIC
PHOTOCOPIABLE

READY RESOURCES ▶▶ GEOGRAPHY

Fishing boats

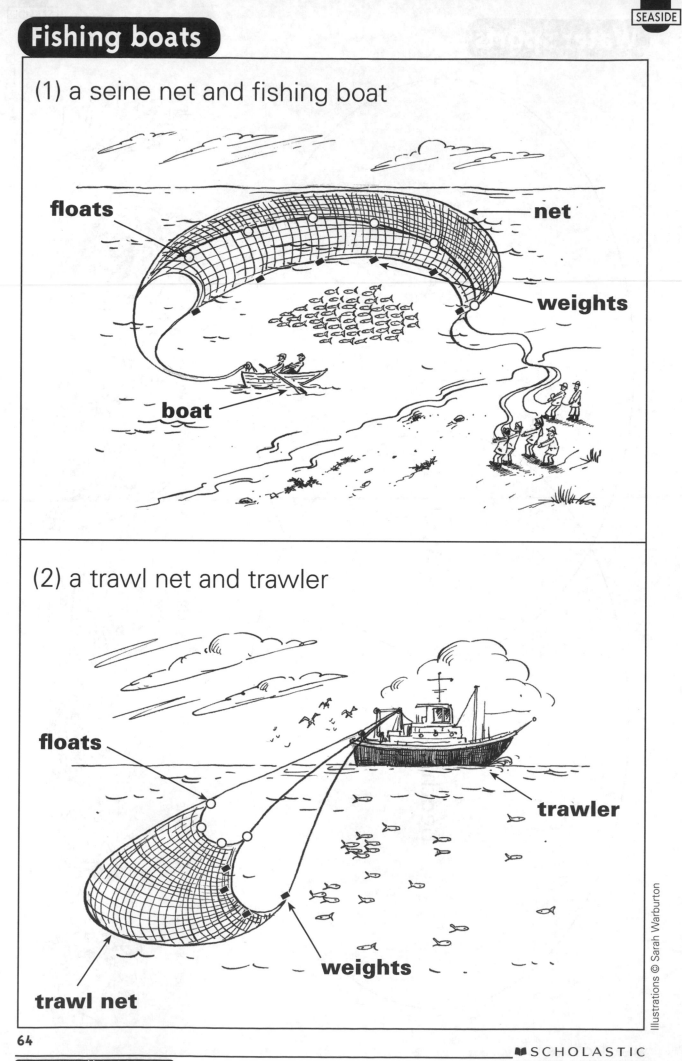

(1) a seine net and fishing boat

floats

net

weights

boat

(2) a trawl net and trawler

floats

trawler

weights

trawl net

Litter on the beach

TRAVELLING TO THE BRITISH ISLES' CAPITALS

Content and skills

This chapter links to unit 5 'Where in the world is Barnaby Bear?' and unit 24 'Passport to the world' of the QCA Scheme of Work for geography at Key Stage 1. The 'Capitals' Resource Gallery on the CD-ROM, together with the teacher's notes and photocopiable pages in this chapter, can be used when teaching these units.

© Photodisc, inc

As with the QCA Scheme of Work, this chapter encourages children to think about their own locality. It also develops their knowledge and understanding of the capitals in the British Isles.

The teacher's notes contain background information about the resources on the CD-ROM and include ways of using them as a whole class, for group work or as individuals. Some of the activities link with other areas of the curriculum, such as literacy and ICT. Wherever possible, the activities encourage the children to ask questions and develop an enquiring approach to their learning.

Resources on the CD-ROM

A plan-view map of the British Isles and the capitals, along with photographs of central and contrasting areas in each of the cities, are provided on the CD-ROM. There are also images that feature a tourist attraction, or major feature, in each capital. These resources can be used as a contrasting locality study for each of the capitals in the British Isles, as well as with a city or town near the children's locality (if appropriate).

Photocopiable pages

The photocopiable pages in the book are also provided in PDF format on the CD-ROM and can be printed from there. They include:
▶ word cards containing essential vocabulary for the unit
▶ an activity sheet that focuses on the sights of London
▶ an activity sheet to develop the children's locational knowledge
▶ an activity sheet on travelling and journey times.

Geographical skills

This chapter identifies opportunities for developing specific geographical skills, including the use of geographical vocabulary, reading and interpreting maps, using secondary sources for further research, and asking and answering geographical questions.

NOTES ON THE CD-ROM RESOURCES

Capitals in the British Isles

For more information on Great Britain and the UK, see page 27.

The five capital cities of the British Isles have all developed on or near river estuaries. Historically, rivers and the sea have been the most economic and practical means of conducting trade. Today, although most goods are moved by road within Britain, most imports and exports are still shipped in and out of Britain's ports.

The capital cities started out as small settlements that grew as people changed from being nomadic to becoming farmers, craftsmen and traders. Capitals are the countries' prime centres for politics, economics and religious affairs.

Discussing the map

▶ Ask the children if they know what a map is and what it can be used for. Explain to the children that the whole geographical area is called the British Isles.

▶ Can the children indicate where land and sea are located on the map?

▶ Go through the names of the different parts of the British Isles with the children.

▶ Explain what a capital city is and show the children the location of each of the capital cities.

Activities

▶ Help the children locate the British Isles on a simple world map.

▶ Explain that Barnaby Bear enjoys travelling around the British Isles. Enlarge the map and display it. Ask the children to bring in a photograph of themselves taken anywhere in the British Isles and add these to the display.

▶ Using the 'Capitals word cards' on photocopiable page 75, ask the children to match the correct capital to the correct position on the map.

LONDON

Central London

This picture shows Selfridges department store on Oxford Street, London. London is one of the largest cities in the world, populated by over seven million people – more people than the individual populations of Scotland, Wales, Northern Ireland, and the Republic of Ireland.

London is also one of the world's most popular tourist destinations with many historical sites, grand buildings, cultural and leisure centres. As a first or second language, English is also more widely spoken than any other.

Discussing the photograph

▶ Ask the children what they can see in the photograph (a busy, wide road, lots of pedestrians, a large, multi-storied building (Selfridges), buses).

▶ As a class, draw a mind map of London.

▶ Explain that London is a cosmopolitan capital and is home to people from different countries and cultures (note the flags on top of Selfridges).

Activities

▶ Let the children colour in flags from around the world. Add these to a world map display.

▶ Let the children cut images of London from holiday brochures. Then ask them to group images. For example, by buildings or transport.

▶ Start a display about capital cities. For each of the five capitals of the British Isles, produce a montage of images in the shape of that city's country.

Westminster

London is the political capital for the whole of the United Kingdom. Politicians meet in the Houses of Parliament, also called Westminster Palace, to debate and pass laws which affect people across England, Scotland, Wales and Northern Ireland. The Houses of Parliament are located on the banks of the River Thames in an area of central London called Westminster.

Discussing the photograph

▶ Ask the children to describe what they can see in the photograph (large, grand buildings (Houses of Parliament), a large clock (Big Ben), a wide river featuring boats and a bridge (the River Thames and Westminster Bridge).

▶ Ask the children if they have heard of the Prime Minister and explain that this building is where important laws are passed by the government.

Activities

▶ Give each child a copy of 'Visiting London' on photocopiable page 78 to complete.

▶ Ask the children which of the places they would like to visit most and why.

Living in Central London

This is a photograph of flats overlooking the Barbican area. London is one of Europe's principle financial centres and provides highly paid employment for many people. High-rise flats are needed to provide housing as land is so limited and expensive. Many modern developments are aimed at people who earn large salaries and do not yet have children.

Discussing the photograph

▶ Discuss what the photograph shows – a series of high-rise flats with little green space.

▶ Explain that this is Central London where there are lots of jobs and where many people live. Also explain that space to build houses is limited, so houses with many storeys are built.

Activities

▶ Ask the children to imagine that they are standing at the top of one of the buildings and to list features they can see below (maybe a water feature or other buildings).

▶ In small groups, let the children build a LEGO version of what can be seen here. Produce an aerial view of their creations by photographing them from above using a digital camera.

Living in London

Before it was possible to build high-rise buildings economically, terracing was the best known way to build good housing within limited land space. This row of Victorian terraces is located within the suburbs of north-west London.

Discussing the picture

▶ Discuss the photograph with the children and note that it shows a suburban location and that the houses look older (period housing).

▶ Explain to the children that a suburb is a residential area outside a city centre.

▶ Point out the cars parked on the street in this photograph. Explain that modern developments in the city centre very often include underground private parking.

Activities

▶ Let the children compare the buildings in this photograph with those in the photograph 'Living in Central London'. What are the main differences?

▶ Show the children the photo of 'Barnaby Bear's house' from the 'Barnaby Bear's local area' Resource Gallery and let them compare Barnaby's house with those in this photograph.

DUBLIN

Central Dublin

Dublin is situated on the east coast of Ireland. It was first established as a town by the Norman Vikings in AD 988. The photograph shows the O'Connell Bridge over the River Liffey. It was built in 1790 to connect the north and south of the city and was previously known as Carlisle Bridge. It was widened in 1880, which led to it being reputed to be as broad as it is long. It was then renamed after Daniel O'Connell, the Irish nationalist leader. His statue stands at the river end of O'Connell Street. This is one of the main streets in Dublin, with the main shopping areas and tourist attractions lying in the north of the city.

Discussing the photograph

▶ Tell the children that this is a photograph of O'Connell Bridge in Dublin and explain that the stretch of water the bridge is crossing is called the River Liffey.

▶ Ask the children to guess what the road from the bridge to the town is called (O'Connell Street). Explain that it was named after a famous Irishman called Daniel O'Connell.

▶ Ask the children to look carefully at the statue standing at the bottom of O'Connell Street. Can they say who this could be a statue of and why.

▶ Can the children identify the buildings along the side of the river? (Restaurants, hotels and pubs.) Explain that there are lots of hotels and restaurants in Dublin because it gets lots of visitors.

Activities

▶ Tell the children that the river often looks green or brown. Ask them to draw pictures of the bridge without clear reflections in the water.

▶ Talk to the children about whether they would like to visit the city. What do they like about it? Use the positive ideas to develop a tourist poster, encouraging Barnaby Bear to visit the city.

▶ Look at a map of Dublin and help the children to find the River Liffey and the O'Connell Bridge.

Dublin Cathedral

Christianity was introduced to Ireland by Saint Patrick in AD 432. This led to the building of many monasteries, particularly around a river estuary known as Dubh Linn (Black Pool). Ireland soon became one of Europe's foremost centres of Christianity and learning. Christ Church Cathedral is Dublin's oldest building and the original wooden church was founded in 1038. The stone church was built by the Anglo-Normans. It was started in 1172 but not finished until several years later. Parts of this building survive today and the current building was restored in the 1870s.

Discussing the photograph

▶ Ask the children to look at the photograph and to suggest what it shows. Tell the children the cathedral's history (see above).

▶ Where do the children think the Norman's found the stone to build the cathedral? (It was probably obtained locally because it would have been difficult to transport from abroad.)

▶ Point out the people on the left. Talk about why tourists might want to visit the cathedral.

▶ Ask the children if they think cars drive under the arch. What clues are there?

Activities

▶ Draw a bird's eye view of the cathedral on a sheet of paper for the children. Why do they think the main part is in the shape of a cross?

▶ Look together at a street map of Dublin and help the children to find the cathedral. Is it the only church in Dublin? What symbols tell the children that buildings are churches or cathedrals?

Living in Dublin

Dublin grew rapidly as a city during Georgian times (a time when four consecutive kings of England, Scotland and Wales were called George). The wealthy had houses built for them in the city centre, and the fashion (Georgian style) was for large terraced houses with plain fronts, brightened up by large, brightly coloured front doors and ornate iron railings. The same style can be found in London and Edinburgh, areas which flourished at this time.

Discussing the photograph

▶ Tell the children that this is a residential street in Dublin, a place where people live. Ask them to look for clues (front doors, window boxes, curtains, no signs above the doors).

▶ Tell the children that these are terraced houses: several houses joined in a row. Ask the children to say where the first house stops and the second one starts. How do they know?

▶ Tell the children that some owners make one house into four flats. Do they think the houses in the photograph have been converted into flats?

▶ Talk about the impact that converting houses into flats has on the area (more people, more cars, more use of services such as water, electricity and rubbish collection).

Activities
▶ Ask the children to draw pictures of Georgian houses. Let them decide whether to keep the front doors white or to choose a different colour.
▶ Ask the children to imagine what they can see out of the upstairs windows. Will they see a road in front of the house or a garden? Ask them to draw pictures of their view.

EDINBURGH

Central Edinburgh

Princes Street is the main shopping street in Edinburgh for clothes, gifts and souvenirs, and is popular with tourists. It divides the Old Town from the New Town and has the Park Street Gardens on one side. It was originally called St Giles Street, but was renamed after the sons of George III. It was once a wealthy residential street with fine views of the Old Town and castle but now it is a busy commercial area with large stores and other shops.

Discussing the photograph
▶ Point out the main street and explain that it is the main shopping street in Edinburgh. Tell the children how the street got its name.
▶ Decide together what sort of street it is. Do people live in the buildings?
▶ Point out the cycle lanes in red alongside the road.
▶ Talk about the yellow crossed section of road, which is used to stop traffic from blocking it. Tell the children that traffic should only go into this if they can keep going to the other side.

Activities
▶ Ask the children to draw a map of the roads and buildings. They can add cycle lanes, double yellow lines and traffic lights to show how to keep the traffic flowing.
▶ Reproduce the street in the classroom with traffic lights, bikes and cars. Let the children take it in turns to ride bikes and drive cars, remembering the rules about driving into the yellow box.
▶ Ask the children to imagine what noises and smells they would experience walking along this street on a busy day.

Edinburgh Castle

No one knows when the Castle Rock was first used as a settlement, but evidence suggests that there was a fort there in Iron Age times. By the 12th century, Edinburgh had become a town and royal burgh. Edinburgh Castle then became the royal residence of Scottish kings and queens. The son of Mary Queen of Scots, James I (James VI of Scotland), was born there. The small chapel at the top of the castle, St Margaret's Chapel, is the oldest part of the castle dating back to Norman times. The castle is now the number one tourist attraction in Scotland, receiving approximately one million visitors every year.

Discussing the photograph
▶ Can the children suggest why the castle is built so high?
▶ Do the children think they would be able to see a long way from the castle? Talk about the distance they would see on a sunny and a foggy day.
▶ Talk about some of the things the children would see from the castle. Focus on the features in the foreground of the photograph, such as cars, churches, shops, houses.
▶ Point out the tower and the Chapel of St Margaret (the small house to the right of the tower.
▶ Can the children say what is flying on top of the tower?

Activities
▶ Introduce the children to the vocabulary to describe the buildings of the castle – moat, mound, tower, chapel and turret.
▶ Ask the children to draw the castle and label the different parts.
▶ Show the children the flag of St Andrew and compare it to the Union Flag. Can the children locate St Andrew's flag on the Union Flag?
▶ In pairs, ask the children to act out a telephone conversation between themselves and a friend, telling them what they liked most about their visit to the castle.

Living in Edinburgh

This photograph was taken from Blackford Hill in autumn sunshine looking toward Edinburgh Castle. It shows clearly a view of the Old Town and its outskirts. Once prosperous, this area suffered from deprivation following the development of the New Town in the 18th century. Its population decreased and those that remained lived in unsanitary conditions. In more recent times, the area has been regenerated and is now looked after by the Old Town Renewal Trust.

Discussing the photograph
▶ Compare the houses in the foreground with those further back. What do the children notice? (Those in the foreground are detached and those in the background are terraced.)
▶ Can the children find the castle in the background? Why does it look smaller than the houses in the foreground of the photograph?

Activities
▶ Compare this photograph with 'Edinburgh Castle' (provided on the CD) and ask the children if the two views are the same. Explain that this photograph shows the back of the castle, while the other shows the front. Make sure they note how the tower and chapel have swapped sides on the photographs.
▶ Ask the children to write an advert for selling one of the houses in the foreground of the photograph. Point out the plus points of living on the outskirts of the city – less noise, fewer smells and better cleanliness.
▶ Look together at a road map and locate the nearest motorway and airport to the city.

CARDIFF

Central Cardiff

Cardiff is the Welsh capital. It is called Caerdydd in Welsh. This photograph shows shoppers in Queen Street, Cardiff's premier shopping street.

The population of Cardiff has remained static over the past 30 years, but the population itself has been gradually changing. In line with other parts of Britain, a growing proportion of the population were born elsewhere.

In 1981, 81 per cent of Cardiff residents were born in Wales, but in 2001 this fell to 75 per cent. However, between 1981 and 2001 the proportion of residents who could speak Welsh rose strongly from 3.5 per cent to 8.8 per cent, while those with a basic knowledge of Welsh rose from 5.7 per cent to 16.3 per cent.

Discussing the photograph
▶ Tell the children that this is the main shopping street in Cardiff.
▶ Introduce the children to the word 'pedestrianisation'. Can they find the signs that tell pedestrians where to go? Point out the walking figure on each sign.
▶ Focus on the windows above the shops. Can the children see any sequence pattern? Tell them that this is because buildings have been divided into several smaller shops.
▶ Point out the symbols on the windows on the right-hand side of the photograph. Do the children think that the upstairs of these shops are used by businesses or to live in?

Activities
▶ Ask the children to compare the shops in the photograph with those near the school. How are they the same or different?
▶ Take the children out to survey the local area for different types of street furniture. Would the children include others to make the area more attractive, such as more litter bins or seats?

Cardiff's Millennium Stadium

The new Millennium Stadium was partly funded by the National Lottery . It was built on the site of the old Cardiff Arms Park stadium, which it replaced as the venue for Welsh international rugby.

The Millennium Stadium is the UK's most modern stadium and is designed to be a multipurpose venue for hosting both sporting events and concerts. It has been used as the venue for the English FA Cup following the closure of London's Wembley Stadium.

The stadium can seat 74,500 spectators and since it opened it has welcomed an average of 1.3 million visitors per year. It has the first retractable roof in the UK.

Discussing the photograph
▶ Explain to the children what the building is. Can they tell you what shape it is?
▶ Talk about the number of people the building will hold. Where do the children think the entrance is? Do they think there is likely to be more than one entrance?
▶ Point out the water around the building. Explain that this is the River Taff.
▶ Ask the children to count the number of times the word Cardiff appears around the outside perimeter. What is the other word written there? (Caerdydd, the Welsh word for Cardiff.)

Activities
▶ Look together at a road map of Cardiff and the surrounding area. Help the children to locate the position of the Millennium Stadium and the River Taff.
▶ Talk about how people travel to the stadium. Do they all come by road? Help the children to locate the airport and railway station on the road map.
▶ Ask the children to pretend that they have been to an event at the stadium. Get them to write a letter home telling their friends what they saw.

Living in Cardiff

Cardiff suffered a decline with the demise of the coal and steel industries. In recent years, however, Cardiff has undergone a major regeneration. This can be seen in the new building and renovation that has taken place across the city. In particular, the Cardiff Bay area, 2km south of the city centre, has been transformed into a high-quality residential, business and leisure location, with transport links into Cardiff city centre and beyond.

This photograph shows the Capitol Building on the development at Adventurers Quay. Within walking distance are the many day- and night-time leisure and shopping facilities built around the waterfront of Cardiff Bay.

Discussing the photograph
▶ Tell the children that this building in Cardiff contains apartments where people live. Explain that there are usually many apartments on the same floor.
▶ Can the children count the number of floors in the building?
▶ Ask the children to think about where residents park their cars. Point out the archways along the bottom of the building through which cars are driven to the underground car park.
▶ Talk about how the area has changed from an industrial area where coal and steel were exported to a more residential area.

Activities
▶ Using the Internet, help the children to find pictures of the Cardiff Bay area. Consider whether it would be a good place to go for a holiday.
▶ Ask the children to consider how they would improve the area. What would they add?
▶ On a large road map, highlight the route cars would take to get to the waterfront. Is this area easy or difficult to find?

BELFAST

Belfast City Airport

Often airports are located more than ten miles from major cities, as they need vast stretches of land for runways and terminals. Belfast has two airports: Belfast International and Belfast City Airport. This photograph shows the City Airport, just two miles out from the city centre. Originally called Belfast Harbour Airport, it was opened in 1938 by the wife of the UK's Prime Minister, Mrs Neville Chamberlain. Shipping ports and airports are very important to Northern Ireland as the country is highly dependent on trade with the rest of the UK, from which it is separated by the Irish Sea.

Low-cost airlines now operate many routes from Belfast to other UK and continental European airports, and this has encouraged people to fly much more often to and from this destination.

Discussing the photograph
▶ Ask the children what they think this building is.
▶ Explain to the children that this photograph was taken in a city called Belfast, the capital city of Northern Ireland.
▶ Explain to the children that this is one of two airports in Belfast and that it is the closest one to the city centre.

Activities
▶ Help the children locate Northern Ireland and Belfast on the 'Capitals in the British Isles' map (provided on the CD).
▶ Give the children a copy of the 'Airline ticket' on photocopiable page 80 and ask them to fill in the questions.
▶ Show the children a photograph of the local airport. Discuss the similarities and differences.

Central Belfast

Of the population in Northern Ireland, 15.9 per cent live in Belfast. It is the natural place for the largest shops to be found. Outside Belfast, agriculture is the most important industry.

Castle Court shopping centre was built in the mid-1990s and is home to a mixture of high street chain stores, found in any UK city. It also accommodates some smaller, local shops.

Discussing the photograph
▶ Explain that this is a central shopping area in Belfast, the capital of Northern Ireland.
▶ Explain to the children that this is a relatively new shopping centre with modern frontages.
▶ Ask the children to guess which season this photograph could have been taken in and to give reasons (such as the clothes people are wearing and the bright sky).

Activities
▶ Ask the children to compare the size of shops in the photograph to those in their own locality.
▶ Show this photograph alongside other photographs of the capitals' central areas (provided on the CD). Which capitals look more modern?

Living in Belfast

Belfast grew rapidly in the 19th century as it became a major industrial centre for textiles (linen) and ship building. Harland and Wolff began building ships, including the infamous Titanic, which sunk on its maiden voyage to New York.

Hundreds of rows of red brick terraced houses were built by the Victorians to house all the people who had moved into Belfast to take jobs in the city's industries. Tight-knit communities formed and partly still remain, as Belfast continues to be the principle centre of employment in Northern Ireland. Thus, people have kept their traditional values, like keeping their doorstep and the road in front of their house clean.

Houses were terraced as they were relatively cheap to build (through sharing adjoining walls and occupying the minimum of land) and enabled large numbers of people to live within walking distance of work. At that time there were no cars or buses.

Discussing the photograph
▶ Discuss the sorts of houses the children live in and ask if anyone lives in a house like the one shown in the photograph (a terraced house).
▶ Explain that capital cities tend to have rows of terraces, which usually look old and period in character.
▶ Explain that modern developers tend to make even better use of restricted space by building high-rise blocks of multiple flats.
▶ Explain why these particular terraces were originally built, focusing on the ship building industry and the degree to which this offered employment, and that historically, employees needed to be able to walk to work.

Activities

▶ Looking at online estate agents' particulars of houses for sale in Belfast and Northern Ireland, and also in the local area, let the children compare building types. Focus on the difference between buildings in cities and suburbs.

▶ Continue with the display on capital cities, asking the children to produce a montage of images of Belfast in the shape of Northern Ireland.

NOTES ON THE PHOTOCOPIABLE PAGES

Word cards   PAGES 75-77

These cards show key words that children will encounter when working on this unit. They include:

▶ words to use for labelling the capital cities and countries of the British Isles on a large map

▶ the names of particular tourist attractions in the capitals, which can be sorted by position and matched to the correct capital city.

Activities

▶ Encourage the children to use the word cards in displays using the maps and pictures in the Resource Gallery, and to help them in talking and writing about the pictures.

▶ Add other words to make a class list as you use the photographs.

Which capital?   PAGE 78

This sheet will encourage the children to remember what they saw in the photographs from the Resource Gallery. Use either the 'Capitals in the British Isles' map (provided on the CD) or a larger one to link each capital with its country.

Activities

▶ Ask the children to list the similarities and differences between the places, including their proximity to water.

▶ Use postcards of other famous tourist spots in the four cities and challenge the children to link these to the correct capital.

▶ Can the children tell you which city and country is missing from the sheet?

Visiting London   PAGE 79

The children will recognise three tourist attractions in London (the Houses of Parliament, Buckingham Palace and St Paul's Cathedral) and think about why people go there.

Activities

▶ Talk through the sheet with the whole class. Which is the most popular place that the children want to visit?

▶ Help the children to look up London on the Internet and find other tourist attractions (Tower Bridge, Tower of London, Piccadilly Circus). Talk about why visitors like to go to these places.

▶ Ask the children to draw pictures of a favourite attraction in London, Dublin, Cardiff, Edinburgh or Belfast to use to make postcards to send home.

Airline ticket   PAGE 80

This sheet encourages the children to consider their own address and how they can get to Belfast in Northern Ireland.

Activities

▶ As a class, identify other airports from where travellers can fly to Belfast. How long does it take to fly from different cities?

▶ Ask the children to consider other ways of getting to Belfast, including ferries.

▶ Show the children a real airline ticket and let them note the information it contains. They could make their own tickets showing travel from your local airport to Belfast.

Capitals word cards

London

Edinburgh

Cardiff

Dublin

Belfast

Capitals word cards

England
Wales
Republic of Ireland
Scotland
Northern Ireland

Capitals word cards

Westminster
Big Ben
Millennium Stadium
Edinburgh Castle
Belfast City Airport
Dublin Cathedral

Which capital?

- Do you know where these places are?

- Did you know that all these capital cities are near water?

Visiting London

• What might you see if you visited London?

What happens here?

_____

_____

_____

What happens here?

_____

_____

_____

What happens here?

_____

_____

_____

• Which of these would you most like to visit and

why? _____

_____

_____

◢SCHOLASTIC
PHOTOCOPIABLE

READY RESOURCES ▶▶ GEOGRAPHY

Airline ticket

Airline You Like

Name: Arthur Smith

Flying from: Manchester Airport

Address: 7 Black Street, Chester, England

Destination: Belfast City Airport

Departure time: 12.30 pm

Seat No: 022C

Arrival time: 1.30 pm

Ticket No: 109365658974

Where is Arthur going?

_____

Which country is he travelling from and to?

_____

How will he get there?

_____

How long will it take?

_____